best ever

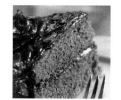

chocolate

p

This is a Parragon Publishing Book
This edition published in 2004

Parragon Publishing
Queen Street House
4 Queen Street
Bath BA1 1HE
United Kingdom

Created and produced by
The Bridgewater Book Company Ltd,
Lewes, East Sussex

Photographer David Jordan
Home economist Judy Williams
Thanks are due to Moulinex and Tower Pans for supplying equipment

ISBN:1-40541-687-4

Printed in China

NOTE

This book uses imperial, metric, or US cup measurements. Follow the same units
of measurement throughout; do not mix imperial and metric. All spoon
measurements are level: teaspoons are assumed to be 5 ml and tablespoons are
assumed to be 15 ml. Unless otherwise stated, milk is assumed to be whole and
eggs and individual fruits such as bananas are medium.

The times given for each recipe are an approximate guide only
because the preparation times may differ according to the techniques used
by different people, and the cooking times may vary as a result of the type of
oven used. Ovens should be preheated to the specified temperature. If using a
fan-assisted oven, check the manufacturer's instructions for adjusting the time
and temperature. The preparation times include cooling, chilling, and freezing
times, where appropriate. Optional ingredients, variations or serving
suggestions have not been included in the calculations.

Recipes using raw or very lightly cooked eggs should be avoided
by infants, the elderly, pregnant women, convalescents, and anyone
suffering from an illness.

contents

introduction

Chocolate seems to have a special power unlike that of any other food. Pharmacists are still not certain what is in the composition of chocolate that makes it quite so irresistible to so many people. To say that consuming chocolate can become an addiction is not an exaggeration, since chocolate contains a natural amphetamine that stimulates the nervous system to produce a feeling of wellbeing, and it also contains theobromine and caffeine, which are both stimulants. Its smooth texture and the fact that it melts at blood temperature make it deliciously seductive.

Few people can resist a chocolate dessert or cake, but tend to think that the art of chocolate cooking is strictly for the experts. This book aims to dispel that myth with recipes that, although they look impressive, do not require any complicated techniques or skills other than a love of good food and a desire to delight family and friends. This collection offers recipes suitable for every occasion, together with ideas for making simple candies and drinks. These opening pages also present a guide to the various types of chocolate and how to choose and store it, as well as simple instructions for melting chocolate and making easy yet effective chocolate decorations.

And there is no need to feel too guilty about eating chocolate, because it is nutritious! It yields up to 600 calories of energy per 3½ oz/100 g, mostly in the form of fat, sugar, protein, and iron. This is why it is included in the survival kits of soldiers and mountaineers.

the history of chocolate

The cacao or cocoa tree has been cultivated since the 7th century and is native to Central and South America. Its botanical name is *Theobroma cacao*, which means "food of the gods."

The chocolate we know today bears little resemblance to xocoatl, the infusion drunk by the Aztecs, Mayans, and Incas. This was extremely bitter and often flavored with spices, including chile. A froth, which was the most desirable part of the drink, was achieved by pouring it from a height. Cacao beans were valued highly and used as currency. Because of its value, chocolate had great ceremonial importance and was served at banquets, offered to the gods and used to anoint newborn babies.

The first Europeans to see the cacao bean were those on Columbus's fourth voyage to the New World in 1502, when he captured a Mayan trading canoe laden with cacao beans and other treasures. However, although he knew of their value as currency, he failed to discover that a drink could be made from them. It was not until 20 years later, when the Spaniards under Cortés invaded Mexico, that the true worth of these black "almonds" was revealed. At first the conquistadores were disgusted by the dark, bitter drink, but they soon learned to appreciate it, especially when they heard rumors of its aphrodisiac qualities. Cortés took some beans with him when he returned home, planting some in Africa on the way. Sugar and milder spices such as vanilla and cinnamon were added and the Spanish quickly became addicted to it. Preachers railed against it from the pulpit, as the ladies were unable to resist sipping it throughout the sermon.

The Spanish King and his court guarded the secret of the delights of chocolate until 1606, when Antonio Carlutti took it to Italy. From then on, the pleasures of drinking chocolate spread quickly across Europe, and Italian cooks started to experiment with adding chocolate as a flavoring in savory and sweet dishes, including sherbets and ice cream.

At the start of the 17th century, this exciting new drink was an expensive luxury appreciated only by the aristocrats of European courts, but soon chocolate houses were springing up all over Europe and they became established as meeting places for fashionable intellectuals. When chocolate houses appeared in London, as predecessors to gentlemen's clubs, they were briefly banned by Charles II as hotbeds of radical politics. The Cocoa Tree Chocolate House, which later became the Garrick Club, was an early headquarters of the Jacobite party, and White's Chocolate House was a headquarters for the Whigs, and later the Tories. These chocolate houses were frequented by Samuel Pepys and many poets, playwrights, and would-be politicians.

The chocolate drink enjoyed at this time was made from a crumbly coarse paste with a high fat content. Two centuries later, a Dutchman called C.J. van Houten developed a screw press that removed the fat or cocoa butter from the beans, leaving a powdery residue, which became known as cocoa. This dispersed easily in water and was considered more digestible than whole chocolate. A use was soon found for the excess cocoa butter when the English firm, Fry & Sons, added sugar and chocolate liquor to the cocoa butter to produce the first eating chocolate. Prices remained high due to the import duty levied on cacao beans, but this was reduced in 1853 and imports of cheap sugar also helped lower the price. Nonetheless, chocolate remained a luxury.

In the early days, all eating chocolate was semisweet with a coarse, grainy texture. The first milk chocolate was made in Switzerland, using dried milk, which was a new product manufactured by Henri Nestlé. Milk and chocolate liquor were mixed and dried, then cocoa butter added, in a process very similar to the modern "milk crumb" process. The Swiss dominated the market for milk chocolate until the early 20th century and continued to improve their recipe until it became the smooth, melting chocolate we know today.

Chocolate became available to a wider audience when it was included in rations for the troops during World War I. After the war, the price of chocolate continued to fall as the price of goods came down and technological advances reduced manufacturing costs. By the start of World War II, chocolate candy was outselling sugar candy—and has continued to do so.

producing chocolate

The cacao tree, *Theobroma cacao*, is cultivated in the tropical zone within 20° of the equator. It requires year-round moisture and a temperature that never falls below 64°F/18°C. West Africa produces 60 percent of the world's supply of cocoa, while Brazil is the largest producer in South America. The trees, which are cultivated under banana or rubber trees to provide shade, start producing pods when they are three to five years old. Although the flowers bloom throughout the year, only about 30 flowers per tree produce red or yellow spindle-shaped pods or fruits, which grow directly out from the trunk. Each pod contains 30–40 white or purple seeds—the cacao beans.

After harvesting, the pods are split open and the contents are scraped out. The seeds and surrounding pulp are piled up on banana or plantain leaves and covered with a layer of damp leaves. They are then left in the sun to ferment for five to six days. As they ferment, the pulp turns to liquid and drains away, and the beans turn a dark brown. This fermentation is essential to allow a good flavor to develop. After fermentation, the beans are left to dry in the sun, then they are exported to the manufacturing country to be turned into the chocolate bars we know and love.

After cleaning, the first stage in processing is roasting, which further develops the cocoa flavor. Then the kernels or "nibs" are extracted from the beans and ground by metal mills with sophisticated temperature controls. The grinding process extracts the cocoa butter, leaving a thick paste—the chocolate liquor. This hardens on cooling to form unsweetened cooking chocolate. Further pressing extracts even more cocoa butter and the solid cake that remains is ground into unsweetened cocoa. To make unsweetened chocolate for eating, extra cocoa butter and sugar are added to the chocolate liquor. Dried milk is added to make milk chocolate.

The next process is known as "conching." The semiliquid mixture is poured into machines that constantly knead the mass at a temperature of 131–185°F/55–85°C. This evaporates moisture, improves the texture and develops the flavor and can take from several hours to a week, depending on the quality required. Toward the end of conching, the desired flavors are added. Vanilla is the most common in European and North American chocolate, but other flavors such as mint, coffee, and orange are also popular.

Before chocolate is molded into bars or used for coating, it is tempered by cooling very carefully to 79°F/26°C. This further improves the texture, gloss, and keeping qualities of chocolate.

types of chocolate

Bitter chocolate is unsweetened chocolate for cooking. It is not widely available but is excellent in baking.

Chocolate couverture is chocolate with a very high cocoa butter content and is generally available only to professional confectioners. It flows very smoothly, making it ideal for coating purposes. It is available in semisweet and milk forms, but is usually expensive.

Semisweet chocolate is the most useful type of chocolate for cooking, as it gives a good strong chocolate flavor. Good-quality chocolate is now widely available in supermarkets. To assess a chocolate's quality, read the label and look for a high cocoa-solid content—the best chocolate contains 50 percent or more. However, chocolate with cocoa solids above 65 percent can be an acquired taste, as they tend to be extremely intense and bitter. Buy the best-quality chocolate you can afford—it will show in the texture, flavor, and appearance of the finished dish. Milk chocolate is not a satisfactory substitute in most recipes, as it is very sweet and does not give such a strong flavor. It is effective piped onto semisweet chocolate for decoration and may be used for molding Easter eggs for children. Look for a cocoa solid content of 40 percent.

White chocolate is not strictly chocolate at all, as it contains cocoa butter, milk, and sugar but no chocolate liquor. It is not normally used in cooking because of its lack of flavor, but its creamy consistency makes it suitable for use in cold desserts, and it makes a good contrast when combined with semisweet chocolate.

Ready-made, chocolate-flavored cake covering is not recommended for the recipes in this book. It contains a minimum of 2.5 percent cocoa solids, and vegetable oil instead of added cocoa butter. It is cheaper than real chocolate, but its flavor and texture are inferior. However, chocolate-flavored cake covering can be easier to use than real chocolate, as it is easier to melt. It is more fluid than melted chocolate, and sets quickly.

Unsweetened cocoa is an inexpensive and convenient way of achieving a strong chocolate flavor in baking, but it is not suitable for use in uncooked dishes, as it has a powdery texture. A good substitute for bittersweet chocolate is to mix together 3 tablespoons of unsweetened cocoa and 1 tablespoon of butter. Add 1 tablespoon of sugar to make a good substitute for semisweet chocolate.

Drinking chocolate is a mixture of unsweetened cocoa and sugar, and is generally too sweet for use in cooking unless the sugar in the recipe is reduced accordingly.

Carob is not chocolate at all, but is a member of the legume family. However, processed carob and chocolate have similarities, so it deserves a mention in this book. Carob is grown all over the Mediterranean and in the United States. The pods, which resemble fava beans, develop into dark brown leathery pods with a glossy surface. The seeds are processed and used as a gelling agent, while the pods are roasted, milled, and strained to produce carob powder, which can be used in cooking. Powdered carob is made into bars by mixing with raw cane sugar, vegetable fats, skim milk powder, lecithin, and flavoring. Carob is rich in vitamins and minerals, contains no refined sugar, theobromine, caffeine, or oxalic acid, and contains fewer calories than chocolate. It can be substituted for chocolate in many recipes, although it will not have the shiny finish of chocolate when melted, and for chocolate-lovers it is no substitute for the real thing!

choosing and storing chocolate

When unwrapped, the surface of chocolate should be glossy and smooth. Semisweet chocolate should be deep mahogany, never black. When you break a bar of chocolate, it should give a crisp snap and there should be a tree-bark texture in the break. When you allow a piece of chocolate to melt on your tongue, it should have a clean taste and the aroma might conjure up caramel, wood, fruit, flowers, or spice. It should be creamy, not oily, and it should melt quickly, which is an indication of a high level of cocoa butter.

When kept in the right conditions, semisweet and milk chocolate will have a shelf life of about one year, but white chocolate tends to deteriorate after about eight months. It should be well wrapped and stored in a cool, dry place, ideally at 61–64°F/16–18°C. "Bloom" is the gray-white coating that appears on the surface of chocolate which has not been stored correctly. Although this looks unattractive, it does not affect the flavor and it is not an indication that the chocolate has "gone off." Chocolate stored at below 55°F/13°C will usually develop a bloom and will "sweat" when returned to room temperature. Chocolate stored at too high a temperature will also develop a bloom.

"Fat bloom" is caused by heating and cooling chocolate. It is quite greasy and rubs off the surface of the chocolate very easily. "Sugar bloom" shows as a white crust of sugar crystals on chocolate that has been stored in a refrigerator.

chocolate in cooking

In European and North American cuisine, chocolate is widely used as a flavoring for desserts, cakes, cookies, and ice cream, and it is often combined with nuts, fruit, orange, mint, coffee, and spirits. In the form of unsweetened cocoa, it provides a concentrated flavor and is used in baking and frostings. Melted block chocolate is used for richer cakes and to flavor creams, mousses, soufflés, sauces, and ice creams.

Chocolate is more usually thought of as an ingredient solely for use in sweet dishes, but it can be used to flavor savory dishes, such as sauce for game and the famous

Mexican mole sauces. It is thought that in Europe it was the Italians who first started using chocolate in savory dishes, such as meat pasties, and it is still used in Italy in the sweet and sour salsa agrodolce, which is served with wild boar and hare. The Spanish took up the idea and there are still Catalan dishes that are seasoned with chocolate. It is used more widely in Latin American dishes, which is a reflection of the Spanish influence.

how to melt chocolate

Chocolate scorches very easily if it is heated above 111°F/44°C, and will "seize" into hard grainy lumps. This will also happen if any liquid or steam comes into contact with the chocolate while it is melting. If the chocolate does seize, there is usually nothing that can be done to make it usable again, but it is worth adding a little oil, which sometimes helps to restore it. Extra care should be taken when melting white chocolate, as it is extremely sensitive to heat.

Chocolate can be safely melted with a small amount of liquid, such as milk, cream, water, or alcohol, if they are placed in the bowl together. It will melt more quickly and evenly if the chocolate is first broken into small pieces. Avoid stirring the chocolate until it has melted and then stir it very gently with a wooden spoon until smooth.

Chocolate can be added to a large quantity of hot liquid and left to melt without stirring. Stir very gently, when completely melted, to make a smooth mixture.

There are several different ways of melting chocolate. The methods described below are the most successful.

Over hot water: break the chocolate into small pieces, then place in a small heatproof bowl and set over a pan of gently simmering water, making sure that the base of the bowl does not come into contact with the water. Remove the pan from the heat and let stand until the chocolate has melted.

In the oven: place the chocolate in a small, shallow ovenproof dish and heat in a preheated oven, 225°F/110°C, until the chocolate has melted.

In a microwave oven: place the chocolate in a microwaveproof bowl and heat for 1–2 minutes in a microwave oven on full power, stirring gently occasionally, until the chocolate has melted. The exact time depends on the quantity of chocolate,

the size of the bowl, and the power of the oven. When melting white chocolate in the microwave, set the oven on 50 percent power and use it in 1 minute bursts, stirring the chocolate at each interval.

In a plastic bag: this is a clean and convenient way of melting a small amount of chocolate, particularly if it is to be used for piping a decoration (see pages 11–12). Place the chocolate in a small plastic food bag, seal and place the bag in a pan of hot water. When the chocolate has melted, cut a corner off the bag and pipe as required.

tips on using melted chocolate

• Let melted chocolate cool slightly before adding to other ingredients.

• Adding a small quantity of butter or oil to the chocolate will make it much smoother and more fluid for coating and dipping.

• Add chocolate to other liquid ingredients rather than pouring the other liquid into the chocolate.

• When using melted chocolate in cake batters, add it to the creamed batter before incorporating the eggs and flour.

• In mousse and soufflé mixtures, blend the melted chocolate with the egg yolks and flavoring before adding the cream and egg whites.

making decorations

When you have gone to all the trouble of making a wonderful chocolate cake or dessert, an attractive decoration will add the finishing touch and make it look all the more professional. Some chocolate decorations can be rather tricky to make at first and will require a little practice before you achieve exactly the desired effect. Others are very easy and straightforward. If you are not very confident, experiment first with chocolate cake covering, as it is easier

to work with than good-quality chocolate. Even if you do have a disaster, you can always re-melt the chocolate and make another attempt. Leave decorations in a cool place to set, but do not put them in the refrigerator or they will develop an unattractive "bloom."

Some of the easiest decorations to make are described below, including chocolate curls, grated chocolate, and chocolate leaves. Half-coating fruit, such as strawberries, is also effective. These not only look good, but taste delicious.

Grated chocolate: This is one of the easiest and most effective chocolate decorations to make at home. Depending on the coarseness of the grater used, a variety of effects, from a fine chocolate powder to coarse curls, can be achieved. Grated chocolate can be sprinkled over a dessert or used to cover the top and sides of a cake that has been coated in cream or buttercream. Alternate lines of grated white and semisweet chocolate can be very attractive as a decoration. Roll homemade truffles in finely grated semisweet, milk, or white chocolate.

Chocolate curls: Use a thick bar of chocolate that has been softened very slightly. It must not be too cold or too warm, and it is only through trial and error that you will achieve the right condition. Run a vegetable peeler down the side of the chocolate bar and allow the curls to fall onto a plate. Lift them carefully onto the cake or dessert that is to be decorated.

Chocolate caraque: Spread a thin layer of melted chocolate onto a flat surface, preferably marble, and just when it appears to have set, but is in fact still soft, hold a knife or scraper at a 45° angle to the surface and push it along to form long scrolls. As the curls form, lift them carefully with the tip of a knife. Caraque may be kept in a box in the refrigerator for a short while, if necessary, until required.

Chocolate leaves: Chocolate leaves are easy to make, and any fresh leaves may be used as long as they are not poisonous. Choose leaves that have prominent veins and are an attractive shape. Rose leaves are ideal. Wash and dry the leaves thoroughly, then brush the underside with melted chocolate. Place the chocolate-coated leaves on a sheet of nonstick parchment paper until completely set, then gently lift the tip of the leaf and peel it away from the chocolate.

Chocolate shapes: For squares, diamonds, and triangles, spread a thin layer of melted chocolate onto a sheet of nonstick parchment paper and leave until just set. Using a ruler and a sharp knife, trim the chocolate into a square, then carefully cut into smaller squares, diamonds, or triangles. Leave in a cool place until completely set before carefully removing from the paper. For other shapes, use a metal cookie or pastry cutter. Aspic cutters are ideal for tiny decorations. These thin chocolate shapes go stale quickly, so they should not be kept for long before use. Because they are very fragile, it is advisable to keep them in an airtight container in the refrigerator. As long as they are left at room temperature to set, and are not stored for long, they are unlikely to develop a bloom.

Chocolate cups: Coat the inside of double-thickness paper cake cases or petit four cases with cooled melted chocolate. Spread the chocolate evenly inside the cases with a brush or spoon. Let set, then add another layer if desired. It is better to brush on two thin layers rather than one thick layer. Leave the cups in a cool place until set hard, then carefully peel away the paper. Chocolate cups make edible containers for fruit and cream, mousse mixtures, or ice cream, and smaller ones can be filled with nuts or truffle mixtures.

Chocolate shells: Large shells make attractive containers for fruit or ice cream and small ones can be used as decorations for cakes and desserts. Cover scallop or other shells with plastic wrap. Brush on a thin, even layer of chocolate. Let set, then brush on a second layer. When completely hard, peel away the plastic wrap.

Piped chocolate: For piping chocolate, use a pastry bag fitted with a fine writing tip or a waxed paper pastry bag. Alternatively, use a small plastic food bag and pipe the chocolate straight from the bag (see page 10). A simple way of achieving a professional finish is to pipe melted chocolate directly onto a cake or dessert. It may be piped as writing or as a pattern. The easiest method is to drizzle randomly. To create a feather design on a cake,

cover the top of a cake with candied frosting and immediately pipe on a spiral of melted chocolate, keeping the rings evenly spaced. Draw the tip of a knife from the edge of the cake to the center, dividing the topping into quarters, then draw the knife from the center to the edge between these lines to create a feathered effect.

Piped decorations: Draw the outline of the shape onto nonstick parchment paper. Pour melted chocolate into a waxed paper pastry bag. Leave for a few seconds to cool and thicken slightly, then snip off the end of the bag and pipe the chocolate round the drawn outlines. Let set, then carefully peel away the paper.

Lacy decorations: Wrap nonstick parchment paper round a rolling pin and drizzle on the chocolate in geometric or swirling patterns with a pastry bag. Do not make them too thin or they will break. When they are set, remove them carefully from the rolling pin.

Lacy chocolate cups: Turn a muffin pan upside down and cover with plastic wrap, pressing it down in between the cups. Pipe a circle round the top and bottom edges of the cups, then pipe a trellis pattern over each cup. When set, remove from the pan.

ready-made decorations

If you don't have the time to make your own chocolate decorations, there is a wide selection of ready-made products available. You don't even have to go to specialist stores to find them, as most supermarkets stock a good range. Some will be found in the home-baking section, while others are from the confectionery section. It is always a good idea to keep a few of these products in the pantry, so that you can instantly enhance the appearance of your cakes and desserts when time is short.

Chocolate chips: These are widely available in semisweet, milk, and white varieties. Chocolate chips can be added to cakes and cookies and will retain their shape when cooked, or they can be used as simple cake decorations. They melt quickly and easily as an alternative to chocolate bars in cooking.

Chocolate buttons: These are very useful as decorations on children's cakes.

Chocolate flake bars: Flakes make an attractive decoration for cakes, drinks, and ice cream. When crumbled, they make an excellent alternative to grated chocolate. Available in milk and white chocolate.

Chocolate vermicelli: Real chocolate vermicelli is not widely available, but the chocolate-coated sugar strands more usually sold as vermicelli are convenient for coating the top and sides of cakes or for sprinkling on ice cream. They can also be used for coating chocolate truffles.

Chocolate leaves: These always look effective on either cakes or desserts.

Chocolate cups and shells: These are available in a variety of sizes and make attractive containers for fruit, ice cream, and mousse mixtures.

basic recipes

rich unsweetened pie dough

makes: 1 x 8-inch/20-cm tart shell
preparation time: 10 mins, plus
1 hr 30 mins chilling

scant 2 cups all-purpose flour, plus
extra for dusting
3½ oz/100 g butter, diced
1 tbsp golden superfine sugar
1 egg yolk, beaten with 1 tbsp water

1 Sift the flour into a large bowl.
Add the butter and rub it in with
your fingertips until the mixture resembles
fine bread crumbs, then stir in the
superfine sugar. Stir in the beaten egg yolk.

2 Knead lightly to form a firm dough.
Cover with plastic wrap and let chill
in the refrigerator for 1 hour 30 minutes.

3 Roll out the dough onto a lightly
floured counter and use to
line an 8-inch/20-cm tart pan. Proceed as
in main recipe.

extra-rich unsweetened pie dough

makes: 8 x 4-inch/10-cm tartlet shells
preparation time: 10 mins,
plus 1 hr chilling

generous 1 cup all-purpose flour, plus
extra for dusting
pinch of salt
3½ oz/100 g butter
1 cup confectioners' sugar
1 large egg, plus 2 large egg yolks

1 Sift the flour and salt into a large
bowl. Make a well in the center
and add the butter, sugar, egg, and yolks.
Using your fingertips, mix the ingredients
in the well into a paste, then gradually
incorporate the flour to make a soft dough.

2 Quickly and lightly knead the
dough, then shape into a ball, wrap
in plastic wrap and chill in the refrigerator
for 1 hour. Proceed as in main recipe.

chocolate pie dough

makes: 1 x 9-inch/23-cm tart shell
preparation time: 10 mins, plus
15 mins chilling

generous 1½ cups all-purpose flour,
plus extra for dusting
2 tbsp unsweetened cocoa
5½ oz/150 g butter
2 tbsp superfine sugar
1–2 tbsp cold water

1 Sift the flour and unsweetened
cocoa into a large bowl. Add the
butter and rub it in with your fingertips
until the mixture resembles fine bread
crumbs. Stir in the superfine sugar and
enough cold water to mix to a soft dough.

2 Cover with plastic wrap and let
chill in the refrigerator for
15 minutes.

3 Roll out the dough on a lightly
floured counter and use to
line a 9-inch/23-cm loose-bottom tart pan.
Proceed as in main recipe.

rich chocolate pie dough

makes: 1 x 8-inch/20-cm deep
tart shell
preparation time: 10 mins,
plus 30 mins chilling

4 tbsp unsweetened cocoa
scant 1½ cups all-purpose flour, plus
extra for dusting
3½ oz/100 g softened butter
4 tbsp superfine sugar
2 egg yolks
few drops of vanilla extract
1–2 tbsp cold water

1 Sift the unsweetened cocoa and
flour into a large bowl. Add the
butter and rub it in with your fingertips
until the mixture resembles fine bread
crumbs. Stir in the superfine sugar. Add the
egg yolks, vanilla extract, and enough
water to mix to a dough.

2 Roll out the dough on a lightly
floured counter and use it
to line a deep 8-inch/20-cm tart or cake
pan. Let chill in the refrigerator for
30 minutes. Proceed as in main recipe.

chocolate sauce

serves: 4
preparation time: 10 mins

3 oz/85 g semisweet chocolate
⅔ cup light cream

1 Break the chocolate into small
pieces and place in a heavy-bottom
pan with the cream. Heat gently,
stirring constantly, until a smooth sauce
is formed.

2 Transfer to a heatproof pitcher
and serve warm.

variation

If you like, you can also add
1 tablespoon of brandy to the
chocolate and cream.

ices & cold desserts

An attractively presented, delicious dessert makes a memorable finale to any meal. Indeed, for many people, it's the highlight of the whole event! The beauty of ices and cold desserts is that they can be made in advance, leaving the cook time to concentrate on the rest of the meal without any last-minute panics in the kitchen. Ice creams and frozen desserts are the most versatile of all, as they can be stored in the freezer and are ready to be produced even if an unexpected guest arrives.

The recipes here range from simple ideas, such as Chocolate Coeurs à la Crème (see page 35) or Chocolate & Orange Pots (see page 45), to the more elaborate for a special occasion, such as Double Chocolate Ice Cream Bombe (see page 17) or Chestnut & Chocolate Terrine (see page 39). But even some of the more complicated recipes, like Zucotto (see page 32) or Tiramisù (see page 54), can be made well in advance, in several manageable stages. Some of the desserts offer the sophisticated flavors of rich dark chocolate and liqueur, such as Iced Chocolate Soufflés (see page 23), while others, such as Chocolate Chip & Fudge Banana Ice Cream (see page 22), make ideal treats for children.

double chocolate ice cream bombe

⏱ **cook: 20 mins**   ⏱ **prep: 50 mins, plus 8–10 hrs freezing**   **serves 6–8**

An ice cream bombe is a spectacular dessert to serve at a dinner party, and the combination of white and dark chocolate is a winner.

---

variation

For a treat, add 2 tablespoons of brandy in the dark chocolate ice cream and 2 tablespoons of Cointreau in the white chocolate.

---

cook's tip

If you do not have a special bombe mold, use a plastic bowl instead. Line it with plastic wrap to make the bombe easier to turn out.

INGREDIENTS

DARK CHOCOLATE ICE CREAM

2 eggs

2 egg yolks

generous ½ cup golden superfine sugar

1¼ cups light cream

8 oz/225 g semisweet chocolate, chopped

1¼ cups heavy cream

WHITE CHOCOLATE ICE CREAM

5 oz/140 g white chocolate, chopped

⅔ cup milk

generous ¼ cup golden superfine sugar

1¼ cups heavy cream

chocolate decorations, to decorate (see pages 10–12)

1 Place a 6-cup/1.5-liter bombe mold in the freezer and set the freezer to rapid freeze. To make the dark chocolate ice cream, follow Steps 1 and 2 of the method for Dark Chocolate Ice Cream on page 18.

2 Freeze in an ice-cream maker, according to the manufacturer's instructions. Alternatively, pour the mixture into a large freezerproof container, then cover and freeze for 2 hours, or until just frozen. Spoon into a bowl and beat with a fork to break down the ice crystals. Return to the freezer until almost solid. Line the bombe mold with the chocolate ice cream and freeze for 2 hours, or until the ice cream is firm.

3 To make the white chocolate ice cream, place the chocolate and half the milk in a pan and heat gently until the chocolate has just melted. Remove from the heat and stir. Place the sugar and remaining milk in a separate pan and heat gently until the sugar has melted. Let cool, then stir into the cooled chocolate mixture. Place the cream in a bowl and whip until lightly thickened, then fold into the chocolate mixture. Spoon into the center of the bombe, then cover and freeze for 4 hours, or until firm. To serve, dip the base of the mold briefly into hot water, then carefully turn out onto a large serving plate and decorate with the chocolate decorations.

dark chocolate ice cream

serves 6   **prep: 25 mins, plus 4 hrs** ↻   **cook: 15 mins** ↻
30 mins freezing/chilling

*This is a serious chocolate ice cream, which appeals more to adult
tastes. However, if you are serving it to children, omit the brandy.*

INGREDIENTS

2 eggs

2 egg yolks

generous ½ cup golden superfine sugar

1¼ cups light cream

8 oz/225 g semisweet
chocolate, chopped

1¼ cups heavy cream

4 tbsp brandy

---

cook's tip

Set the freezer to its coldest setting
about 1 hour before you intend to
freeze the mixture and remember to
return the freezer to its normal
setting afterward.

1 Place the whole eggs, egg yolks, and sugar in a heatproof bowl and beat together until well blended. Place the light cream and chocolate in a pan and heat gently until the chocolate has melted, then continue to heat, stirring constantly, until almost boiling. Pour onto the egg mixture, stirring vigorously, then set the bowl over a pan of gently simmering water, making sure that the base of the bowl does not touch the water.

2 Cook, stirring constantly, until the mixture lightly coats the back of the spoon. Strain into a separate bowl and let cool. Place the heavy cream and brandy in a separate bowl and whip until slightly thickened, then fold into the cooled chocolate mixture.

3 Freeze in an ice-cream maker, following the manufacturer's instructions. Alternatively, pour the mixture into a large freezerproof container, then cover and freeze for 2 hours, or until just frozen. Spoon into a bowl and beat with a fork to break down the ice crystals. Return to the freezer for 2 hours, or until firm. Transfer the ice cream to the refrigerator 30 minutes before serving. Scoop the ice cream into 4 serving dishes or coffee cups and serve.

marbled chocolate & orange ice cream

cook: 15 mins

prep: 15 mins, plus 10 hrs 30 mins freezing/chilling

serves 6

Swirls of orange-flavored chocolate run through the white chocolate and not only look attractive but taste delicious too.

cook's tip

To make this into a mint ice cream, use good-quality mint-flavored semisweet chocolate instead of the orange-flavored semisweet chocolate, if you like.

INGREDIENTS

6 oz/175 g white chocolate

1 tsp cornstarch

1 tsp vanilla extract

3 egg yolks

1¼ cups milk

2 cups heavy cream

4 oz/115 g orange-flavored semisweet chocolate, broken into pieces

grated orange rind, to decorate

orange segments, to serve

1 Using a sharp knife, chop the white chocolate into small pieces and set aside. Place the cornstarch, vanilla extract, and egg yolks in a heatproof bowl and beat together until well blended. Pour the milk into a large, heavy-bottom pan and bring to a boil over low heat. Pour over the egg yolk mixture, stirring constantly.

2 Strain the mixture back into the pan and heat gently, stirring constantly, until thickened. Remove from the heat, add the white chocolate pieces and stir until melted. Stir in the cream. Set aside ⅔ cup of the mixture and pour the remainder into a large freezerproof container. Cover and freeze for 2 hours, or until starting to set. Melt the orange-flavored chocolate (see pages 9–10), stir into the reserved mixture and set aside.

3 Remove the partially frozen ice cream from the freezer and beat with a fork. Place spoonfuls of the orange chocolate mixture over the ice cream and swirl with a knife to give a marbled effect. Freeze for 8 hours, or overnight, until firm. Transfer to the refrigerator 30 minutes before serving. Scoop into individual glasses, decorate with orange rind, and serve with a few orange segments.

coconut & white chocolate ice cream

serves 6 **prep: 25 mins, plus 5 hrs** ⏲ 30 mins freezing/chilling   **cook: 15 mins** ⏲

Coconut and white chocolate combine to make a smooth, creamy ice cream with an exotic flavor. Perfect for a hot summer's day.

INGREDIENTS

2 eggs

2 egg yolks

generous ½ cup golden superfine sugar

1¼ cups light cream

4 oz/115 g white chocolate, chopped

4 oz/115 g creamed coconut, chopped

1¼ cups heavy cream

3 tbsp coconut rum

tropical fruit, such as mango, pineapple, or passion fruit, to serve

---

variation

As an alternative to serving with fruit, this ice cream is also delicious served with a chocolate sauce (see page 13) poured over the top.

---

cook's tip

To make serving the ice cream easier, dip the ice-cream scoop briefly in a small bowl of hot water before serving each portion. If you don't have an ice-cream scoop, a serving spoon will be just as good.

1 Place the whole eggs, egg yolks, and sugar in a heatproof bowl and beat together until well blended. Place the light cream, chocolate, and coconut in a pan and heat gently until the chocolate has melted, then continue to heat, stirring constantly, until almost boiling. Pour onto the egg mixture, stirring vigorously, then set the bowl over a pan of gently simmering water, making sure that the base of the bowl does not touch the water.

2 Heat the mixture, stirring constantly, until it lightly coats the back of the spoon. Strain into a clean, heatproof bowl and let cool. Place the heavy cream and rum in a separate bowl and whip until slightly thickened, then fold into the cooled chocolate mixture.

3 Freeze in an ice-cream maker, following the manufacturer's instructions. Alternatively, pour the mixture into a large freezerproof container, then cover and freeze for 2 hours, or until just frozen. Spoon into a bowl and beat with a fork to break down the ice crystals. Return to the freezer for 3 hours, or until firm. Transfer the ice cream to the refrigerator for 30 minutes before serving. Scoop into small serving bowls and serve with tropical fruit.

chocolate chip & fudge banana ice cream

serves 6   **prep: 15 mins, plus 6 hrs ⟳ 15 mins freezing/chilling**   **cook: 0 mins ⟳**

This indulgent ice cream is equally popular with both adults and children and makes a wonderful midweek dessert.

INGREDIENTS

4 ripe bananas

juice of ½ lemon

1 cup golden superfine sugar

generous 2 cups whipping cream

generous ½ cup semisweet chocolate chips

3½ oz/100 g fudge, cut into small pieces, plus extra to decorate

cook's tip

Choose bananas that are ripe but not brown. It is important to add lemon juice as the juice helps to prevent the bananas from turning brown.

1 Peel the bananas and chop them coarsely, then place in a food processor with the lemon juice and sugar. Process until well chopped, then pour in the cream and process again until well blended.

2 Freeze in an ice-cream maker, following the manufacturer's instructions, adding the chocolate chips and fudge just before the ice cream is ready. Alternatively, pour the mixture into a large freezerproof container, then cover and freeze for 2 hours, or until just frozen. Spoon into a bowl and beat with a fork to break down the ice crystals. Return the ice cream to the freezer for an additional 2 hours, or until almost firm. Remove from the freezer, beat again with a fork, and stir in the chocolate chips and fudge. Return to the freezer for an additional 2 hours, or until firm.

3 Transfer the ice cream to the refrigerator 15 minutes before serving. Scoop into small bowls and decorate with extra fudge pieces. Serve.

iced chocolate soufflés

cook: 5 mins   **prep: 30 mins, plus 8 hrs freezing**   **serves 6**

Individual iced soufflés look very special, and make serving easier too! For an elegant presentation, decorate with chocolate curls.

cook's tip

When whisking egg whites, make sure the bowl is dry, spotlessly clean and free from any grease, otherwise the whites will not hold their shape.

INGREDIENTS

3½ oz/100 g semisweet chocolate, chopped

1 tbsp instant coffee powder

2 tbsp water

4 eggs, separated

1 cup confectioners' sugar, sifted

1 cup heavy cream

2 tbsp Tia Maria

Chocolate Curls (see page 10), to decorate

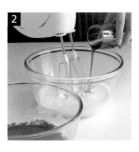

1 Tie a double band of foil tightly round each of 6 ramekins, to stand 1 inch/2.5 cm above the rim. Place the chocolate, coffee powder, and water in a small pan and heat gently until melted. Let cool slightly.

2 Place the egg yolks and confectioners' sugar in a bowl. Beat with an electric whisk until thick and light. Whisk in the melted chocolate mixture. Place the cream and Tia Maria in a separate bowl and whip until thick. Set aside.

3 Whisk the egg whites in a separate, clean, greasefree bowl until stiff but not dry. Stir 1 tablespoon of the whisked egg whites into the chocolate mixture, then gently fold in the remaining egg whites with the cream. Pour into the ramekins and freeze for 8 hours, or overnight. Remove the foil carefully. Decorate the soufflés with chocolate curls and serve.

italian chocolate christmas pudding

⏱ cook: 5 mins   ⏲ prep: 15 mins, plus 8 hrs chilling   serves 10

This pudding is a wonderful alternative for anyone who dislikes a traditional Christmas pudding, but there is absolutely no reason why it should be served only at Christmas!

variation

For a change, substitute the amaretti cookies with crushed graham crackers and replace the amaretto liqueur with the same amount of brandy.

cook's tip

As this pudding is very rich, it should be cut into very thin slices. To make it easier to slice, dip a sharp knife into hot water and wipe away any excess water before slicing.

INGREDIENTS

butter, for greasing

½ cup mixed candied fruit, chopped

⅓ cup raisins

grated rind of ½ orange

3 tbsp orange juice

3 tbsp light cream

12 oz/350 g semisweet chocolate, chopped

½ cup cream cheese

4 oz/115 g amaretti cookies, broken into coarse pieces

TO SERVE

½ cup whipping cream

2 tbsp amaretto liqueur

1 oz/25 g semisweet chocolate, grated

1 Grease a 3½-cup/850-ml ovenproof bowl with butter. Place the candied fruit, raisins, orange rind, and juice in a bowl and mix together. Put the light cream and chocolate in a pan and heat gently until the chocolate has melted. Stir until smooth, then stir in the fruit mixture. Let cool.

2 Place the cream cheese and a little of the chocolate mixture in a large bowl and beat together until smooth, then stir in the remaining chocolate mixture. Stir in the broken amaretti cookies. Pour into the prepared bowl, cover with plastic wrap and let chill in the refrigerator overnight.

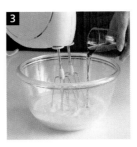

3 To serve, turn the pudding out onto a chilled serving plate. Pour the whipping cream into a bowl and add the amaretto liqueur. Whip lightly until slightly thickened. Pour some of the cream over the pudding and sprinkle grated chocolate over the top. Serve with the remaining cream.

chocolate sherbet

prep: 15 mins, plus ⏱ 9 hrs freezing/chilling

cook: 10 mins ⏱

This chocolate sherbet makes a light and refreshing yet luxurious end to any meal. It is especially good served with some crisp cookies and freshly brewed coffee.

INGREDIENTS

½ cup unsweetened cocoa

generous ¾ cup golden superfine sugar

2 tsp instant coffee powder

2 cups water

crisp cookies, to serve

cook's tip

Making the sherbet in an ice-cream maker will give the best results. If you do not have one, beat the sherbet frequently while it is freezing to help make it light and smooth.

 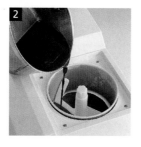 

1 Sift the unsweetened cocoa into a small, heavy-bottom pan and add the superfine sugar, coffee powder, and a little of the water. Using a wooden spoon, mix together to form a thin paste, then gradually stir in the remaining water. Bring the mixture to a boil over low heat and let simmer gently for 8 minutes, stirring frequently.

2 Remove the pan from the heat and let cool. Transfer the mixture to a bowl, cover with plastic wrap and place in the refrigerator until well chilled. Freeze in an ice-cream maker, following the manufacturer's instructions. Alternatively, pour the mixture into a large freezerproof container, then cover and freeze for 2 hours. Remove the sherbet from the freezer and beat to break down the ice crystals. Freeze for an additional 6 hours, beating the sherbet every 2 hours.

3 Transfer the sherbet to the refrigerator 30 minutes before serving. Scoop into 6 small bowls and serve with crisp cookies.

chocolate kulfi

cook: 20 mins **prep: 1 hr, plus 10 hrs freezing** **serves 6**

Kulfi is a delicately spiced Indian ice cream traditionally made in tube-shaped terracotta containers. Although chocolate is not an authentic ingredient, it makes this ice cream even more of a treat.

cook's tip

Use a wide, heavy-bottom pan for reducing the milk to allow plenty of room for the liquid to bubble up. This will help to speed up the evaporation.

INGREDIENTS

2 quarts creamy milk

12 whole cardamom pods

⅜ cup golden superfine sugar

3½ oz/100 g semisweet chocolate, chopped

2 tsp blanched almonds, chopped

¼ cup shelled unsalted pistachios, chopped

1 Place the milk and cardamom pods in a large, heavy-bottom pan. Bring to a boil over low heat, then let simmer vigorously until reduced to one-third of its original amount.

2 Strain the milk into a heatproof bowl, discarding the cardamom pods, then stir in the sugar and chocolate until melted. Add the almonds and half the pistachios, then let cool. Pour the mixture into a large freezerproof container, then cover and freeze for 2 hours, or until almost firm, stirring every 30 minutes.

3 Pack the ice cream into 6 yogurt pots or dariole molds, cover with plastic wrap and freeze for 8 hours, or until completely solid. To serve, dip the base of the molds briefly into hot water, then turn out onto dessert plates. Sprinkle over the remaining pistachios to decorate and serve.

chocolate banana sundae

serves 4 **prep: 15 mins** ⏱ **cook: 5 mins** 🍲

A banana split in a glass! Choose the best-quality vanilla ice cream you can find, or, better still, if you have time make your own.

INGREDIENTS

SAUCE	SUNDAE
2 oz/55 g semisweet chocolate	4 bananas
4 tbsp corn syrup	⅔ cup heavy cream
1 tbsp butter	8–12 scoops of good-quality vanilla
1 tbsp brandy or rum (optional)	ice cream
	generous ⅜ cup slivered or chopped
	almonds, toasted
	grated or flaked chocolate,
	for sprinkling
	4 fan wafer cookies, to serve

variation

For a traditional banana split, halve the bananas lengthwise and place on a plate with 2 scoops of ice cream. Top with cream, nuts, and chocolate sauce.

cook's tip

When melting chocolate in a heatproof bowl set over a pan of simmering water, make sure that the bowl does not touch the water.

1 To make the sauce, break the chocolate into small pieces and place in a heatproof bowl with the syrup and butter. Place the bowl over a pan of hot water and heat until melted, stirring constantly, until well blended. Remove from the heat and stir in the brandy or rum, if using.

2 Peel and slice the bananas. Place the cream in a large bowl and whip until just holding its shape. Place a scoop of ice cream in the bottom of 4 tall sundae dishes, then top with slices of banana, some sauce, a spoonful of cream, and a generous sprinkling of nuts.

3 Repeat the layers, finishing with a generous spoonful of cream, sprinkled with nuts and a little grated chocolate. Serve with fan wafer cookies.

baked chocolate alaska

⏲ **cook: 12 mins**   ⏱ **prep: 50 mins**   **serves 4**

*A very cool dessert that leaves the cook completely unflustered—
assemble it in advance and just freeze until required.*

---

variation

Try adding a layer of mixed canned fruit on top of the sponge, then top with the ice cream and meringue. Proceed as in main recipe.

---

cook's tip

This dessert is delicious served with a black currant coulis. Cook a few black currants in a little orange juice until soft, purée, and push through a strainer, then sweeten to taste with a little confectioners' sugar.

INGREDIENTS

butter, for greasing

2 eggs

4 tbsp superfine sugar

5 tbsp all-purpose flour

2 tbsp unsweetened cocoa

3 egg whites

generous ¾ cup superfine sugar

4 cups good-quality chocolate ice cream

4

5

6

1 Preheat the oven to 425°F/220°C. Grease a 7-inch/18-cm round cake pan with butter and line the bottom with parchment paper.

2 Whisk the eggs and the 4 tablespoons of sugar in a bowl until very thick and pale. Sift the flour and cocoa together and fold in.

3 Pour into the prepared pan and bake in the preheated oven for 7 minutes, or until springy to the touch. Transfer to a wire rack to cool.

4 Whisk the egg whites in a spotlessly clean, greasefree bowl until soft peaks form. Gradually add the sugar, whisking, until you have a thick, glossy meringue.

5 Place the sponge on a large baking sheet and pile the ice cream in the center in a heaped dome.

6 Pipe or spread the meringue over the ice cream, making sure that the ice cream is completely enclosed. (At this point the dessert can be frozen, if you like.)

7 Return to the oven for 5 minutes, or until the meringue is just golden. Serve immediately.

zucotto

serves 6

prep: 30 mins, plus
7–9 hrs chilling/cooling

cook: 15–20 mins

Zucotto is a traditional Italian dessert that combines those natural partners, semisweet chocolate and black cherries.

INGREDIENTS

4 oz/115 g soft margarine, plus
extra for greasing

scant ⅔ cup self-rising flour

2 tbsp unsweetened cocoa

½ tsp baking powder

generous ½ cup golden superfine sugar

2 eggs, beaten

3 tbsp brandy

2 tbsp Kirsch

FILLING

1¼ cups heavy cream

¼ cup confectioners' sugar, sifted

¼ cup toasted almonds, chopped

8 oz/225 g black cherries, pitted

2 oz/55 g semisweet chocolate,
finely chopped

TO DECORATE

1 tbsp unsweetened cocoa

1 tbsp confectioners' sugar

fresh cherries

variation

If fresh cherries are not available, use drained canned cherries instead. Replace the Kirsch with an almond-flavored liqueur, such as amaretto.

cook's tip

If the zucotto is thoroughly chilled beforehand it can be left unmolded for a couple of hours at the table, making it ideal to serve as part of a buffet lunch.

1 Preheat the oven to 375°F/190°C. Grease a 12 x 9-inch/30 x 23-cm jelly roll pan with margarine and line with parchment paper. Sift the flour, cocoa, and baking powder into a bowl. Add the sugar, margarine, and eggs. Beat together until well mixed, then spoon into the prepared pan. Bake in the preheated oven for 15–20 minutes, or until well risen and firm to the touch. Let stand in the pan for 5 minutes, then turn out onto a wire rack to cool.

2 Using the rim of a 5-cup/1.2-litre ovenproof bowl as a guide, cut a circle from the cake and set aside. Line the bowl with plastic wrap. Use the remaining cake, cutting it as necessary, to line the bowl. Place the brandy and Kirsch in a small bowl and mix together. Sprinkle over the cake, including the reserved circle.

3 To make the filling, pour the cream into a separate bowl and add the confectioners' sugar. Whip until thick, then fold in the almonds, cherries, and chocolate. Fill the sponge mold with the cream mixture and press the cake circle on top. Cover with a plate and a weight, and let chill in the refrigerator for 6–8 hours, or overnight. When ready to serve, turn the zucotto out onto a serving plate. Decorate with cocoa and confectioners' sugar, sifted over in alternating segments, and a few cherries.

chocolate coeurs à la crème

cook: 0 mins　　　　**prep: 20 mins, plus 8 hrs chilling**　　　　**serves 8**

This is a delicious adaptation of a classic French dessert, traditionally made in pierced heart-shaped porcelain molds.

---

variation

Other types of fresh berries would work equally well as a coulis. Try black currants or blackberries, if they are in season.

---

cook's tip

As in this recipe, substitute pierced yogurt pots in place of the authentic porcelain molds. Top with halved fresh strawberries for the *coeur* or heart shape.

INGREDIENTS

generous 1 cup ricotta cheese

½ cup confectioners' sugar, sifted

1¼ cups heavy cream

1 tsp vanilla extract

2 oz/55 g semisweet chocolate, grated

2 egg whites

COULIS

1 cup fresh raspberries

confectioners' sugar, to taste

TO DECORATE

fresh strawberries, halved

fresh raspberries

1 Line 8 individual molds with cheesecloth. Press the ricotta cheese through a strainer into a bowl. Add the confectioners' sugar, cream, and vanilla extract and beat together thoroughly. Stir in the grated chocolate. Place the egg whites in a separate clean bowl and whisk until stiff but not dry. Gently fold into the cheese mixture.

2 Spoon the mixture into the prepared molds. Stand the molds on a tray or dish and let drain in the refrigerator for 8 hours, or overnight—the cheesecloth will absorb most of the liquid.

3 To make the raspberry coulis, place the raspberries in a food processor and process to a purée. Press

the purée through a strainer into a bowl and add confectioners' sugar, to taste. To serve, turn each dessert out onto a serving plate and pour the raspberry coulis round. Decorate with strawberries and raspberries, then serve.

chocolate rum creams

**prep: 10 mins, plus
2 hrs cooling/chilling**

cook: 5 mins

*This dessert requires no cooking apart from warming the cream,
and is extremely easy to make. It is particularly good served with
crisp cookies and makes a superb finale to a dinner party menu.*

INGREDIENTS

3½ oz/100 g semisweet chocolate,
broken into pieces

⅔ cup light cream

1¼ cups whipping cream

1 tbsp confectioners' sugar, sifted

2 tbsp white rum

Chocolate Curls (see page 10),
to decorate

cook's tip

This dessert looks particularly attractive
served in matching tall glasses. You
can also use coffee cups, or ordinary
dessert dishes would work just as well.

1 Place the chocolate and
light cream in a small,
heavy-bottom pan and heat
very gently until the chocolate
has melted. Stir until smooth,
then remove from the heat
and let cool. Pour the
whipping cream into a large
bowl and, using an electric
whisk, whip until thick but
not stiff.

2 Carefully whisk the
cooled sugar, rum, and
chocolate mixture into the
whipped cream. Take care not
to overwhisk.

3 Spoon the mixture into
6 serving dishes or
glasses, cover with plastic wrap
and let chill in the refrigerator
for 1–2 hours.

4 Make the chocolate
curls and sprinkle them
carefully over the creams
before serving.

chocolate & strawberry brûlées

cook: 8 mins   **prep: 15 mins, plus 2 hrs 30 mins freezing/thawing**   **serves 6**

Fresh fruit covered with a delicious chocolate cream and crunchy caramelized topping couldn't be easier to make, yet it is impressive enough to serve at any dinner party.

cook's tip

Freezing the brûlées before broiling ensures that the cream will not bubble up through the sugar, but if short of time, it is not necessary to freeze them. You can caramelize the sugar with a culinary blowtorch.

INGREDIENTS

scant 1¼ cups fresh strawberries, washed and hulled

2 tbsp fruit liqueur, such as Kirsch or crème de cassis

2 cups heavy cream

4 oz/115 g semisweet chocolate, melted and cooled (see pages 9–10)

½ cup firmly packed raw brown sugar

TO DECORATE

fresh strawberries

fresh mint leaves

1 Cut the strawberries into halves or quarters, depending on their size, and divide between 6 ramekins. Sprinkle with the fruit liqueur.

2 Pour the cream into a bowl and whip until it is just holding its shape. Add the cooled chocolate and continue whipping until the cream is thick. Spread over the strawberries. Cover and place in the freezer for 2 hours, or until the cream is frozen.

3 Preheat the broiler to high. Sprinkle the sugar thickly over the cream, then place under the hot broiler and cook until the sugar has melted and caramelized. Let the brûlées stand for 30 minutes, or until the fruit and cream have thawed. Serve decorated with a few fresh strawberries and mint leaves.

black & white pudding

serves 4–6   prep: 30 mins, plus ⏲ 30 mins cooling   cook: 45 mins ⏲

This rich dessert is a cross between a steamed pudding and a soufflé. It makes an extravagant treat whatever the occasion.

INGREDIENTS

oil, for brushing

4 oz/115 g unsalted butter

generous ½ cup golden superfine sugar

½ tsp ground cardamom seeds

4 eggs, separated

4 oz/115 g semisweet chocolate, melted and cooled (see pages 9–10)

1 tbsp rum

⅔ cup heavy cream

¼ cup crème fraîche or sour cream

variation

Instead of the cream and crème fraîche, serve with fresh summer berries, such as raspberries and black currants and vanilla ice cream.

1 Lightly brush a 3½-cup/850-ml ovenproof bowl with oil. Place the butter, sugar, and cardamom in a bowl and beat until light and thick. Gradually beat in the egg yolks. Carefully stir in the cooled chocolate and the rum. Place the egg whites in a separate, spotlessly clean, greasefree bowl and whisk until stiff but not dry.

2 Stir 1 tablespoon of the whisked egg whites into the chocolate mixture, then carefully fold in the remainder.

Turn the mixture into the prepared bowl. Cover with oiled parchment paper and foil and tie securely with string. Place the bowl in a large, heavy-bottom pan and pour in enough boiling water

to come one-third of the way up the side of the bowl. Cover the pan and let simmer gently for 45 minutes.

3 Leave the pudding in the bowl until cold, then turn out onto a serving dish. Whip the cream and crème fraîche together until thick. Cover the pudding with the cream or serve separately.

chestnut & chocolate terrine

cook: 5 mins   **prep: 30 mins, plus 8 hrs chilling**   **serves 6**

Chestnut and chocolate is an all-time classic combination and it is experienced at its best in this delicious layered terrine.

variation

You can substitute Marsala wine or dry sherry for the rum, if you would prefer a different flavor.

INGREDIENTS

¾ cup heavy cream

4 oz/115 g semisweet chocolate, melted and cooled (see pages 9–10)

generous ⅓ cup rum

1 package rectangular, plain, sweet cookies

8 oz/225 g canned sweetened chestnut purée

unsweetened cocoa, for dusting

confectioners' sugar, to decorate

1 Line a 1-lb/450-g loaf pan with plastic wrap. Place the cream in a bowl and whip lightly until soft peaks form. Using a spatula, fold in the cooled chocolate.

2 Place the rum in a shallow dish. Lightly dip 4 cookies into the rum and arrange on the bottom of the pan. Repeat with 4 more

cookies. Spread half the chocolate cream over the cookies. Make another layer of 8 cookies dipped in rum and spread over the chestnut purée, followed by another layer of cookies. Spread over the remaining chocolate cream and top with a final layer of cookies. Cover with plastic wrap and let chill for 8 hours, or preferably overnight.

3 Turn the terrine out onto a large serving dish. Dust with unsweetened cocoa. Cut strips of paper and place these randomly on top of the terrine. Sift over confectioners' sugar. Carefully remove the paper. To serve, dip a sharp knife in hot water, dry it, and use it to cut the terrine into slices.

chocolate & hazelnut parfait

cook: 10 mins

prep: 30 mins, plus 8 hrs 20 mins cooling/freezing

serves 6

Richly flavored, molded ice creams make a truly scrumptious summertime dessert for all the family.

variation

Replace the blanched hazelnuts with other types of nuts, such as macadamias, almonds, or Brazil nuts, if you prefer.

cook's tip

Melt chocolate slowly and gradually as it easily burns and becomes unusable. As soon as the chocolate has melted, remove the pan from the heat.

INGREDIENTS

generous 1 cup blanched hazelnuts

6 oz/175 g semisweet chocolate, broken into small pieces

2½ cups heavy cream

3 eggs, separated

2¼ cups confectioners' sugar

1 tbsp unsweetened cocoa, for dusting

6 small fresh mint sprigs, to decorate

wafer cookies, to serve

1 Preheat the broiler to medium. Place the hazelnuts on a baking sheet and toast under the broiler for 5 minutes until golden. Cool.

2 Place the chocolate in a heatproof bowl and set over a pan of simmering water until melted. Cool. Place the hazelnuts in a food processor and process until ground.

3 Whisk the cream until stiff, then fold in the hazelnuts. Beat the egg yolks with 3 tablespoons of the sugar for 10 minutes, or until pale and thick.

4 Whisk the egg whites in a clean, greasefree bowl until soft peaks form. Whisk in the remaining sugar, a little at a time, until the whites are stiff and glossy. Stir the cooled chocolate into the egg yolk mixture, then fold in the cream. Fold in the egg whites. Divide the mixture between 6 freezerproof molds, cover with plastic wrap, and freeze for at least 8 hours until firm.

5 Transfer the parfaits to the refrigerator 10 minutes before serving to soften slightly. Turn out onto 6 serving plates, dust the tops lightly with cocoa, decorate with mint sprigs, and serve with wafers.

chocolate terrine with orange cream

serves 10–12

prep: 30 mins, plus 3 hrs chilling

cook: 10 mins

Contrasting bands of white, milk, and dark chocolate look stunning when this terrine is sliced and surrounded with orange cream.

INGREDIENTS

6 tbsp water

3 tsp powdered gelatin

4 oz/115 g each of milk, white, and semisweet chocolate, broken into pieces

2 cups whipping cream

6 eggs, separated

scant ⅜ cup superfine sugar

ORANGE CREAM

2 tbsp superfine sugar

1 tbsp cornstarch

2 egg yolks

⅔ cup milk

⅔ cup heavy cream

grated rind of 1 orange

1 tbsp Cointreau

orange juice (optional)

TO DECORATE

⅔ cup heavy cream, whipped

chocolate-covered coffee beans

orange zest

variation

As an alternative to the orange cream, simply serve the terrine with some pouring cream, if you like.

cook's tip

When lining a terrine or loaf pan with plastic wrap, make sure that there is a generous overhang, so you can use it to cover the top before freezing.

1 Line a 5-cup/1.2-liter terrine or loaf pan with plastic wrap. To make the milk chocolate mousse, place 2 tablespoons of the water in a heatproof bowl. Sprinkle on 1 teaspoon of gelatin and let stand for 5 minutes. Set the bowl over a pan of simmering water until the gelatin has dissolved. Cool. Melt the milk chocolate (see pages 9–10)

and cool. Whip one-third of the cream until thick. Whisk 2 of the egg whites in a bowl until stiff but not dry. Whisk 2 of the egg yolks and one-third of the sugar in a separate bowl until thick. Stir in the chocolate, dissolved gelatin, and whipped cream. Fold in the whisked egg whites. Pour into the pan. Cover and freeze for 20 minutes, or until set.

2 Make the white chocolate mousse in the same way, pour over the milk chocolate mousse and freeze. Make the semisweet chocolate mousse and pour on top. Chill for 2 hours, until set.

3 To make the orange cream, stir the sugar, cornstarch, and egg yolks together until smooth. Heat

the milk, cream, and orange rind in a pan until almost boiling, then pour over the egg mixture, whisking. Strain back into the pan and heat until thick. Cover and let cool. Stir in the Cointreau. The cream should be runny; if not, stir in a little orange juice. Turn out the terrine. Decorate with cream, coffee beans, and orange zest. Serve with the orange cream.

white chocolate mousse

serves 6   prep: 15 mins, plus 8 hrs chilling   cook: 8 mins

White chocolate makes a sweet and creamy mousse, and fragrant rose water adds an interesting flavor.

INGREDIENTS

9 oz/250 g white chocolate, broken into pieces

generous ⅓ cup milk

1¼ cups heavy cream

1 tsp rose water

2 egg whites

4 oz/115 g semisweet chocolate, broken into pieces

candied rose petals, to decorate

variation

Instead of spreading semisweet chocolate on top of the mousses, spoon black currant or black cherry jelly on top, if you like.

1 Place the white chocolate and milk in a pan and heat gently until the chocolate has melted, then stir. Transfer to a large bowl and let cool.

2 Place the cream and rose water in a separate bowl and whip until soft peaks form. Whisk the egg whites in a separate spotlessly clean, greasefree bowl until stiff but not dry. Gently fold the whipped cream into the chocolate, then fold in the egg whites. Spoon the mixture into 6 small dishes or glasses, cover with plastic wrap and let chill for 8 hours, or overnight, to set.

3 Melt the semisweet chocolate (see pages 9–10) and let cool, then pour evenly over the mousses. Let stand until the chocolate has hardened, then decorate with rose petals and serve.

chocolate & orange pots

cook: 5 mins

prep: 15 mins, plus 1 hr chilling

serves 8

These little pots of rich chocolate cream will satisfy the most serious chocolate-lovers. They look superb served in matching coffee cups.

cook's tip

Let the chocolate pots chill in the refrigerator for no more than 2 hours, otherwise the mixture becomes too firmly set in the ramekins or cups.

INGREDIENTS

7 oz/200 g semisweet chocolate, broken into pieces

grated rind of 1 orange

1¼ cups heavy cream

¾ cup golden superfine sugar

3 tbsp Cointreau

3 large egg whites

fine strips of orange rind, to decorate

crisp cookies, to serve

1 Melt the chocolate (see pages 9–10) and stir in the orange rind. Place the cream in a bowl with ½ cup of the sugar and the Cointreau and whip until thick.

2 Place the egg whites in a separate, spotlessly clean, greasefree bowl and whisk until soft peaks form, then gradually whisk in the remaining sugar until stiff but not dry. Fold the melted chocolate into the cream, then beat in a spoonful of the whisked egg whites. Gently fold in the remaining egg whites until thoroughly mixed.

3 Spoon the mixture into 8 small ramekins or demi-tasse coffee cups. Cover and let chill in the refrigerator for 1 hour, then decorate with a few strips of orange rind before serving with crisp cookies.

oeufs à la neige au chocolat

cook: 15–20 mins

prep: 15 mins, plus
2 hrs chilling

serves 6

In this dessert, poached meringues float on a richly flavored chocolate custard like little snowballs.

variation

You can also drizzle caramel over the top. Dissolve 2 tablespoons of sugar in 3 tablespoons of water in a pan and boil until a caramel has formed.

cook's tip

Cook the custard over a low heat and do not let it boil as it will curdle and separate. If it does start to curdle, remove the pan from the heat and strain the custard into a cold bowl.

INGREDIENTS

2½ cups milk

1 tsp vanilla extract

scant ⅞ cup superfine sugar

2 egg whites

unsweetened cocoa, for dusting

CUSTARD

4 tbsp superfine sugar

3 tbsp unsweetened cocoa

4 egg yolks

1 Place the milk, vanilla extract, and 5 tablespoons of the sugar in a heavy-bottom pan and stir over low heat until the sugar has dissolved. Simmer gently.

2 Whisk the egg whites in a spotlessly clean, greasefree bowl until stiff peaks form. Whisk in 2 teaspoons of the remaining sugar and continue to whisk until glossy. Gently fold in the rest of the sugar.

3 Drop large spoonfuls of the meringue mixture onto the simmering milk mixture and cook, stirring once, for 4–5 minutes, or until the meringues are firm. Remove with a slotted spoon and let drain on paper towels.

Poach the remaining meringues in the same way, then set aside the milk mixture.

4 To make the custard, mix the sugar, cocoa, and egg yolks in the top of a double boiler or in a heatproof bowl. Gradually whisk in the reserved milk mixture. Place over a pan of barely simmering water and cook for 5–10 minutes, whisking constantly, until thickened. Remove from the heat and let cool slightly. Divide the chocolate custard between 6 serving glasses and top with the meringues. Cover and let chill in the refrigerator for at least 2 hours. When ready to serve, dust the tops of the meringues with cocoa.

chocolate mint swirl

serves 6   **prep: 15 mins, plus** ⟲ **30 mins cooling/setting**   **cook: 5 mins** ⏲

The classic combination of chocolate and mint flavors makes an attractive dessert for all kinds of special occasions.

INGREDIENTS

1¼ cups heavy cream

⅔ cup creamy mascarpone cheese

2 tbsp confectioners' sugar

1 tbsp crème de menthe

6 oz/175 g semisweet chocolate

2 oz/55 g semisweet chocolate,

to decorate

---

variation

For a chocolate orange swirl, replace the crème de menthe with the same amount of Cointreau.

---

cook's tip

Pipe the patterns freehand or draw patterns onto parchment paper, turn the paper over and pipe the chocolate, following the drawn outline.

1 Place the cream in a large bowl and whip until soft peaks form.

2 Fold in the mascarpone cheese and sugar, then place one-third of the mixture in a smaller bowl. Stir the crème de menthe into the small bowl. Melt the chocolate (see pages 9–10) and stir it into the remaining mixture.

3 Place alternate spoonfuls of the 2 mixtures into serving glasses, then swirl the mixture together to give a decorative effect. Let cool, then let chill in the refrigerator until required.

4 To make the piped chocolate decorations, melt a small amount of chocolate (see pages 9–10)

and place in a paper pastry bag. Place a sheet of parchment paper on a board and pipe squiggles, stars, or flower shapes with the melted chocolate. Alternatively, pipe decorations onto a long strip of parchment paper, then place the strip over a rolling pin, securing with sticky tape. Let set, then remove from the parchment paper.

5 Decorate each dessert with piped chocolate decorations and serve. The desserts can be decorated and chilled in the refrigerator, if you like.

coffee panna cotta with chocolate sauce

cook: 10 mins

prep: 25 mins, plus 8 hrs chilling

serves 6

Panna cotta literally means "cooked cream." Flavoring it with coffee and serving it with a chocolate sauce adds a new look to this popular Italian dessert.

variation

For a special occasion, use heart-shaped molds lined with plastic wrap for easy removal. They are available from most kitchen stores.

cook's tip

Individual metal ovenproof bowl molds are ideal for these desserts—the panna cotta turns out more easily than from china molds.

INGREDIENTS

oil, for brushing

2½ cups heavy cream

1 vanilla bean

generous ¼ cup golden superfine sugar

2 tsp instant espresso coffee granules, dissolved in 4 tbsp water

2 tsp powdered gelatin

chocolate-covered coffee beans, to serve

SAUCE

⅔ cup light cream

2 oz/55 g semisweet chocolate, melted (see pages 9–10)

1 Lightly brush 6 x ⅔-cup/150-ml molds with oil. Place the cream in a pan. Split the vanilla bean and scrape the black seeds into the cream. Add the vanilla bean and the sugar, then heat gently until almost boiling. Strain the cream into a heatproof bowl and set aside. Place the coffee in a small heatproof bowl, sprinkle on the gelatin and let stand for 5 minutes, or until spongy. Set the bowl over a pan of gently simmering water until the gelatin has dissolved.

2 Stir a little of the reserved cream into the gelatin mixture, then stir the gelatin mixture into the remainder of the cream. Divide the mixture between the prepared molds and let cool, then let chill in the refrigerator for 8 hours, or overnight.

3 To make the sauce, place one-quarter of the cream in a bowl and stir in the melted chocolate. Gradually stir in the remaining cream, reserving 1 tablespoon. To serve the panna cotta, dip the base of the molds briefly into hot water and turn out onto 6 dessert plates. Pour the chocolate cream round. Dot drops of the reserved cream onto the sauce and feather it with a toothpick. Decorate with chocolate-covered coffee beans and serve.

mocha creams

cook: 5 mins

prep: 10 mins, plus 20 mins standing/setting

serves 4

These delicious creamy chocolate- and coffee-flavored desserts make a perfect end to any dinner party meal.

variation

To add a delicious almond flavor to the dessert, replace the coffee-flavored liqueur with amaretto, an almond-flavored liqueur.

cook's tip

Always whip cream in a large bowl as the cream will double in volume. If using an electric mixer, always start whipping slowly and gradually increase the speed.

INGREDIENTS

8 oz/225 g semisweet chocolate

1 tbsp instant coffee

1¼ cups boiling water

1 envelope gelatin

3 tbsp cold water

1 tsp vanilla extract

1 tbsp coffee-flavored liqueur (optional)

1¼ cups heavy cream

4 chocolate-covered coffee beans

8 amaretti cookies, to serve

1 Break the chocolate into small pieces and place in a pan with the coffee. Stir in the boiling water and heat gently, stirring, until the chocolate has melted.

2 Sprinkle the gelatin over the cold water and let stand for 5 minutes, or until spongy, then whisk it into the chocolate to dissolve it.

3 Stir in the vanilla extract and coffee-flavored liqueur, if using. Let stand in a cool place until just starting to thicken, whisk occasionally.

4 Whip the cream until soft peaks form, then set aside a little for decorating the desserts and fold the remainder into the chocolate mixture. Spoon into 4 serving dishes and let set. Decorate with the reserved cream and coffee beans and serve with amaretti cookies.

tiramisù

serves 8 **prep: 30 mins, plus 3 hrs chilling** **cook: 30 mins**

Tiramisù is an Italian version of trifle. A wicked combination of mascarpone cheese, chocolate, coffee, and rum makes this delicious dessert very rich and quite irresistible!

INGREDIENTS

butter, for greasing

3 eggs

¾ cup golden superfine sugar

⅔ oz self-rising flour

1 tbsp unsweetened cocoa

⅔ cup cold black coffee

2 tbsp rum

2 tsp unsweetened cocoa, to decorate

FILLING

1⅝ cups mascarpone cheese

1 cup fresh custard

¼ cup golden superfine sugar

3½ oz/100 g semisweet chocolate, grated

variation

To save time, use ladyfingers instead of cake. Dip them in coffee and layer them with the mascarpone cheese mixture in a bowl.

cook's tip

Remove the mascarpone cheese from the refrigerator 30 minutes before using, to let it soften. This makes it easier to beat and to blend with the superfine sugar.

1 Preheat the oven to 350°F/180°C. To make the cake, grease an 8-inch/20-cm round cake pan with butter and line with parchment paper. Place the eggs and sugar in a large bowl and beat together until thick and light. Sift the flour and unsweetened cocoa over the batter and fold in gently. Spoon the batter into the prepared pan and bake in the oven for 30 minutes, or until the cake springs back when pressed gently in the center. Let stand in the tin for 5 minutes, then turn out onto a wire rack to cool.

2 Place the black coffee and rum in a bowl or cup, mix together and set aside. To make the filling, place the mascarpone cheese in a large bowl and beat until soft. Stir in the custard, then gradually add the sugar, beating constantly. Stir in the grated chocolate.

3 Cut the cake horizontally into 3 layers and place 1 layer on a serving plate. Sprinkle with one-third of the coffee mixture, then cover with one-third of the mascarpone mixture. Repeat the layers, finishing with a topping of the mascarpone mixture. Let chill in the refrigerator for 3 hours. Sift over the unsweetened cocoa before serving.

chocolate & amaretto cheesecake

cook: 1 hr 10 mins   **prep: 30 mins, plus 3 hrs chilling**   **serves 10–12**

Amaretto is an almond-flavored Italian liqueur, which complements the semisweet chocolate and cream in this cheesecake perfectly.

variation

If you do not have any amaretto liqueur, use another liqueur, such as Cointreau or brandy, instead.

cook's tip

To loosen the cheesecake, use a round-bladed knife to run round the inside, as a sharp knife may damage both the cake and the pan.

INGREDIENTS

oil, for brushing
6 oz/175 g graham crackers
2 oz/55 g amaretti cookies
3 oz/85 g butter

FILLING
8 oz/225 g semisweet chocolate
1¾ cups cream cheese, at room temperature
generous ½ cup golden superfine sugar

3 tbsp all-purpose flour
1 tsp vanilla extract
4 eggs
1¼ cups heavy cream
¼ cup amaretto liqueur

TOPPING
1 tbsp amaretto liqueur
¾ cup crème fraîche or sour cream
crushed amaretti cookies

1 Line the bottom of a 9-inch/23-cm springform cake pan with foil and brush the sides with oil. Place the graham crackers and amaretti cookies in a plastic bag and crush with a rolling pin. Place the butter in a pan and heat until just melted, then stir in the crushed cookies. Press the mixture into the bottom of the pan and let chill for 1 hour.

2 Preheat the oven to 325°F/160°C. To make the filling, melt the chocolate (see pages 9–10) and let cool. Place the cream cheese in a bowl and beat until fluffy, then add the sugar, flour, and vanilla extract and beat together until smooth. Gradually add the eggs, beating until well blended. Blend in the melted chocolate, cream, and amaretto liqueur. Pour the mixture over the chilled biscuit base and bake in the oven for 50–60 minutes, or until set.

3 Leave the cheesecake in the oven with the door slightly ajar, until cold. Run a knife round the inside of the pan to loosen the cheesecake. Let chill in the refrigerator for 2 hours, then remove from the pan and place on a serving plate. To make the topping, stir the amaretto liqueur into the crème fraîche and spread over the cheesecake. Sprinkle the crushed amaretti cookies round the edge to decorate.

marbled chocolate cheesecake

serves 10–12 **prep: 45 mins, plus 3 hrs chilling** **cook: 1 hr 10 mins**

Cheesecake is always a favorite dessert, and this one, with marbled swirls of semisweet and white chocolate, is particularly appealing. It is perfect for an extra special occasion.

INGREDIENTS

oil, for brushing
8 oz/225 g semisweet chocolate graham crackers

FILLING
3 oz/85 g butter
1 lb 9 oz/700 g cream cheese
scant 1 cup golden superfine sugar

3 tbsp all-purpose flour
2 tsp vanilla extract
3 eggs, beaten
4 oz/115 g semisweet chocolate, broken into pieces
4 oz/115 g white chocolate, broken into pieces

variation

A ginger-flavored base would also work well—substitute gingersnaps for the semisweet chocolate graham crackers.

cook's tip

Although it will take longer for the cheesecake to be ready, leaving it to cool in the oven with the door slightly ajar helps to prevent cracks appearing on the surface. Remove the cheesecake when it is completely cold.

1 Line the bottom of a 9-inch/23-cm springform cake pan with foil and brush the sides with oil. Place the graham crackers in a plastic bag and crush with a rolling pin. Place the butter in a pan and heat gently until just melted, then stir in the crushed crackers. Press into the bottom of the pan and let chill in the refrigerator for 1 hour.

2 Preheat the oven to 325°F/160°C. To make the filling, place the cream cheese in a bowl and beat until fluffy, then add the sugar, flour, and vanilla extract and beat together until smooth. Gradually add the eggs, beating until well blended. Place half the mixture in a separate bowl. Melt the semisweet chocolate and white chocolate in 2 separate bowls (see pages 9–10) and let cool. Stir the semisweet chocolate into one bowl of cream cheese mixture and the white chocolate into the other.

3 Spoon the 2 mixtures alternately over the chilled cracker base, then swirl with a knife to give a marbled effect. Bake in the preheated oven for 50–60 minutes, or until set. Leave the cheesecake in the oven with the door slightly ajar, until cold. Run a knife round the inside of the pan to loosen the cheesecake. Let chill in the refrigerator for 2 hours before removing from the pan to serve.

irish cream cheesecake

serves 12   **prep: 45 mins, plus 3 hrs chilling**   **cook: 10 mins**

This is an unbaked cheesecake, and although it is not set with gelatin, its high chocolate content ensures that it sets perfectly.

INGREDIENTS

oil, for brushing
6 oz/175 g chocolate chip cookies
2 oz/55 g butter

FILLING

8 oz/225 g semisweet chocolate
8 oz/225 g milk chocolate
¾ cup golden superfine sugar
1½ cups cream cheese
1¾ cups heavy cream, whipped
3 tbsp Irish cream liqueur

TO SERVE

crème fraîche or sour cream
fresh fruit

---

cook's tip

Look out for miniature bottles of Irish cream liqueur, as they are a handy size for cooking. If you cannot find Irish cream liqueur, try using brandy.

1 Line the bottom of an 8-inch/20-cm springform cake pan with foil and brush the sides with oil. Place the cookies in a plastic bag and crush with a rolling pin. Place the butter in a pan and heat gently until just melted, then stir in the crushed cookies. Press the mixture into the bottom of the pan and let chill in the refrigerator for 1 hour.

2 To make the filling, melt the semisweet and milk chocolate together (see pages 9–10), stir to combine and let cool. Place the sugar and cream cheese in a large bowl and beat together until smooth, then fold in the whipped cream. Fold the mixture gently into the melted chocolate, then stir in the Irish cream liqueur.

3 Spoon the filling over the chilled biscuit base and smooth the surface. Cover and let chill in the refrigerator for 2 hours, or until quite firm. Transfer to a serving plate and cut into small slices. Serve with a spoonful of crème fraîche or sour cream and fresh fruit.

chocolate wafer layers

⏱ **cook: 5 mins**

🕐 **prep: 50 mins, plus 30 mins–60 mins chilling**

serves 6

Crisp delicate wafers of chocolate layered with a rich pistachio cream filling taste as impressive as they look.

cook's tip

Try not to overbeat the mascarpone cheese filling otherwise it will become quite runny and difficult to spread over the chocolate wafers.

INGREDIENTS

6 oz/175 g semisweet chocolate, broken into pieces

1⅛ cups mascarpone cheese

1 tbsp superfine sugar

4 tbsp Tia Maria

1¼ cups heavy cream

¾ cup shelled, unsalted pistachios, chopped

4 oz/115 g milk chocolate, grated

1 Melt the chocolate (see pages 9–10) and let cool. Cut 6 strips of nonstick parchment paper measuring 2½ x 10½ inches/6 x 27 cm. Brush evenly with the melted chocolate. Mark each strip with a knife every 3½ inches/ 9 cm to make rectangles. Let set in the refrigerator, then carefully peel off the chocolate wafers.

2 Place the mascarpone cheese and sugar in a bowl and beat together until smooth. Beat in the Tia Maria and cream until soft peaks form. Fold in the pistachios and grated milk chocolate.

3 Arrange 6 chocolate wafers on a baking sheet and spoon over half the mascarpone cheese mixture. Lay a second wafer on top of each one and cover with the remaining mixture. Top with a final chocolate wafer. Let chill in the refrigerator until ready to serve.

chocolate brandy torte

 cook: 10 mins   prep: 40 mins, plus   serves 12
                       2 hrs chilling

A crumbly ginger chocolate base topped with velvety smooth
chocolate brandy cream makes this a blissful cake.

---

variation

If chocolate-covered coffee beans are
unavailable, use chocolate-coated
raisins to decorate instead.

---

cook's tip

When folding cream into the
chocolate, do not overwork the
mixture by mixing it too much as you
want a light and fluffy end result.

INGREDIENTS

BASE

3½ oz/100 g butter, plus extra
for greasing

9 oz/250 g gingersnaps

2¾ oz/75 g semisweet chocolate

FILLING

8 oz/225 g semisweet chocolate

generous 1 cup mascarpone cheese

2 eggs, separated

3 tbsp brandy

1¼ cups heavy cream

4 tbsp superfine sugar

TO DECORATE

generous ⅓ cup heavy cream

chocolate-covered coffee beans

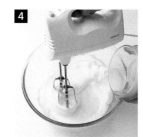

1 Grease the bottom and sides of a 9-inch/23-cm springform cake pan. Place the gingersnaps in a plastic bag and crush with a rolling pin. Transfer to a bowl. Place the chocolate and butter in a small pan and heat gently until melted, then pour over the cookies. Mix well, then press into the prepared pan. Let chill while preparing the filling.

2 To make the filling, place the chocolate in a heatproof bowl and set over a pan of simmering water, stirring, until melted. Remove from the heat and beat in the mascarpone cheese, egg yolks, and brandy.

3 Whip the cream until just holding its shape. Fold in the chocolate mixture.

4 Whisk the egg whites in a spotlessly clean, greasefree bowl until soft peaks form. Add the sugar, a little at a time, and whisk until thick and glossy. Fold into the chocolate mixture, in 2 batches, until just mixed.

5 Spoon the mixture into the prepared base and let chill in the refrigerator for at least 2 hours. Carefully transfer to a serving plate. To decorate, whip the cream and pipe onto the cheesecake, add the chocolate-covered coffee beans, and serve.

rich chocolate loaf

makes 16 slices

prep: 20 mins, plus 1 hr chilling

cook: 5 mins

Another rich chocolate dessert, this loaf is very simple to make and can be served as a teatime treat as well.

INGREDIENTS

½ cup almonds

5½ oz/150 g semisweet chocolate

6 tbsp unsalted butter

scant 1 cup sweetened condensed milk

2 tsp ground cinnamon

2¾ oz/75 g amaretti cookies, broken

generous ¼ cup no-soak dried apricots, coarsely chopped

cook's tip

To melt chocolate, first break it into manageable pieces. The smaller the pieces, the quicker it will melt. Remember to remove from the heat as soon as it has melted.

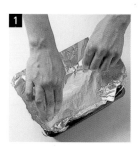

1 Line a 1 lb 8-oz/675-g loaf pan with a piece of foil. Using a sharp knife, coarsely chop the almonds and set aside until required.

2 Place the chocolate, butter, milk, and cinnamon in a small heavy-bottom pan and heat over low heat for 3–4 minutes, stirring constantly with a wooden spoon, or until the chocolate has melted. Remove from the heat and beat the mixture until well blended.

3 Stir the chopped almonds, cookies, and apricots into the chocolate mixture with a wooden spoon until thoroughly mixed.

4 Pour the mixture into the prepared pan and let chill in the refrigerator for 1 hour, or until set. Cut the loaf into slices to serve.

mississippi mud pie

⏲ **cook: 1 hr 10 mins**   ⏱ **prep: 30 mins, plus 4 hrs cooling/chilling**   **serves 8**

An all-time favorite with chocoholics—the "mud" refers to the gooey, rich chocolate layer of the cake.

cook's tip

To make sure the dough cooks evenly and does not become too soggy, it is usually baked blind before the filling is added. Line with foil or parchment paper and use dried beans or pie weights to hold it down.

INGREDIENTS

1 quantity of Basic Chocolate Pie Dough (see page 13)

all-purpose flour, for dusting

6 oz/175 g butter

generous 1⅛ cups dark brown sugar

4 eggs, lightly beaten

4 tbsp unsweetened cocoa, sifted

5½ oz/150 g semisweet chocolate

1¼ cups light cream

1 tsp chocolate extract

TO DECORATE

scant 2 cups heavy cream, whipped

Chocolate Curls and Chocolate Flakes (see pages 10–12)

1 Preheat the oven to 375°F/190°C. Make the pie dough (see page 13) and let chill for 15 minutes. Roll out the dough on a lightly floured counter and use to line a deep 9-inch/23-cm loose-bottom tart pan. Line the case with foil and dried beans or pie weights, then bake blind in the preheated oven for 15 minutes. Remove the beans and foil

and cook for an additional 10 minutes, or until the pastry shell is crisp.

2 To make the filling, beat the butter and sugar together in a large bowl and gradually beat in the eggs with the cocoa. Melt the chocolate (see pages 9–10) and beat it into the mixture with the cream and chocolate extract.

3 Reduce the oven temperature to 325°F/160°C. Pour the mixture into the cooked pastry shell and bake in the oven for 45 minutes, or until the filling is set.

4 Let the pie cool completely, then transfer to a large serving plate. Cover with the whipped cream

and let chill in the refrigerator for 1 hour. Decorate the pie with Chocolate Curls and Chocolate Flakes and let chill in the refrigerator for 2 hours before serving.

chocolate chiffon pie

serves 8   **prep: 35 mins, plus 4 hrs 30 mins cooling/chilling**   **cook: 12–15 mins**

The nutty crust of this delectable pie contrasts with the tempting creamy chocolate filling. Serve with cream, if you like.

INGREDIENTS

2 tbsp chopped Brazil nuts, plus extra to decorate

2 tbsp granulated sugar

2 tsp melted butter

1 cup milk

2 tsp gelatin

generous ½ cup superfine sugar

2 eggs, separated

8 oz/225 g semisweet chocolate, coarsely chopped

1 tsp vanilla extract

⅔ cup heavy cream

variation

If you like, replace the nut base with either a Chocolate Cookie Base (see page 60) or a Rich Chocolate Pie Dough (see page 13).

cook's tip

When dissolving gelatin in a bowl set over a pan of simmering water, do not let the gelatin mixture boil or overheat, otherwise the gelatin will become stringy and may spoil the finished dessert.

1 Preheat the oven to 400°F/200°C. Place the nuts in a food processor and process until finely ground. Add the granulated sugar and butter and process briefly. Transfer the mixture to a 9-inch/23-cm round springform cake pan and press it onto the bottom and sides with a spoon. Bake for 8–10 minutes, or until golden. Cool.

2 Pour the milk into the top of a double boiler or into a heatproof bowl and sprinkle the gelatin on the top. Let soften for 2 minutes, then place over a pan of simmering water. Stir in half the superfine sugar, both the egg yolks, and all the chocolate. Stir over low heat for 4–5 minutes, or until the gelatin has dissolved and the chocolate has melted.

Remove from the heat and beat until smooth and blended. Stir in the vanilla extract, cover, and let chill in the refrigerator for 45–60 minutes, or until just starting to set.

3 Whip the cream until stiff, then fold all but 3 tablespoons into the chocolate mixture. Whisk the egg whites in a spotlessly clean bowl until soft peaks form. Add 2 teaspoons of the remaining superfine sugar and whisk until stiff peaks form. Fold in the remaining sugar, then fold the egg whites onto the chocolate mixture. Pour the filling onto the base and let chill for 3 hours, or until set. Decorate the pie with the remaining whipped cream and the chopped nuts before serving.

chocolate trifle

cook: 10 mins

prep: 45 mins, plus 2 hrs 30 mins cooling/chilling

serves 8

This is a wonderful dessert for a party. It makes a change from a conventional trifle, and is served with chocolate truffles and fruit.

variation

If you like, replace the raspberry jelly with black currant jelly and use mixed berries, such as black currants and raspberries, to decorate.

cook's tip

Frozen packages of fruit are available in most supermarkets. Sometimes they are described as "summer fruits" or "fruits of the forest." Try to find a variety that includes cherries.

INGREDIENTS

10 oz/280 g ready-made chocolate loaf cake
3–4 tbsp seeded raspberry jelly
4 tbsp amaretto liqueur
9 oz/250 g package frozen mixed red fruit, thawed

CUSTARD
6 egg yolks
generous ¼ cup golden superfine sugar
1 tbsp cornstarch
2 cups milk
2 oz/55 g semisweet chocolate, melted (see pages 9–10)

TOPPING
1 cup heavy cream
1 tbsp golden superfine sugar
½ tsp vanilla extract

TO DECORATE
ready-made chocolate truffles
fresh fruit, such as cherries and strawberries

1 Cut the cake into slices and make "sandwiches" with the raspberry jelly. Cut the sandwiches into cubes and place in a large serving bowl. Sprinkle with the amaretto liqueur. Spread the fruit over the cake.

2 To make the custard, place the egg yolks and sugar in a heatproof bowl and whisk until thick and pale, then stir in the cornstarch. Place the milk in a pan and heat until almost boiling. Pour onto the egg yolk mixture, stirring. Return the mixture to the pan and bring just to a boil, stirring constantly, until it thickens. Remove from the heat and let cool slightly. Stir in the melted chocolate. Pour the custard over the cake and fruit. Let cool, then cover and let chill in the refrigerator for 2 hours, or until set.

3 To make the topping, whip the cream until soft peaks form, then beat in the sugar and vanilla extract. Spoon over the trifle. Decorate with truffles and fruit and let chill until ready to serve.

hot desserts

Because so few people these days either eat or cook desserts on a regular basis, they tend to be regarded as something of a treat. Nothing is guaranteed to please your family and friends more than the sight of a hot chocolate pudding at the end of a meal! Despite the fact that many of these hot desserts are actually easier to prepare than elaborate chilled desserts, your guests will feel extra pampered and indulged when they are served these homemade delights.

Some of the following recipes are based on tried-and-trusted favorites, but with an added dimension, such as Chocolate Bread & Butter Pudding (see page 86) and Steamed Chocolate Pudding (see page 96), while dishes like Chocolate Fondue (see page 77), Baked Peaches with Chocolate (see page 73), and Barbecued Chocolate Bananas (see page 80) are deceptively simple to make. Others, such as Exotic Fruit Chocolate Crêpes (see page 74) and Chocolate Cake with Rosemary Custard (see page 92) are full of exotic and fragrant flavors. Many of the desserts can be made in advance and reheated just before serving, and none require elaborate decoration or presentation. So give your guests something really special, and sit back and enjoy the compliments!

ginger pears with chocolate sauce

serves 4   **prep: 20 mins**   **cook: 20–25 mins**

Pears and chocolate form another highly successful partnership in this simple dessert that is extremely easy to make.

INGREDIENTS

4 dessert pears

2 cups water

generous ¾ cup golden superfine sugar

4-inch/10-cm piece fresh gingerroot, peeled and sliced

½ cinnamon stick

dash of lemon juice

SAUCE

4 tbsp light cream

7 oz/200 g semisweet chocolate, broken into pieces

cook's tip

Choose unblemished dessert pears that are ripe but still firm, so that they keep their shape when cooked. Suitable varieties include Comice and Anjou pears.

1 Peel the pears, leaving the stalks intact. Cut the base of each pear so that it sits upright. Carefully remove as much of the core as possible with a small spoon.

2 Place the water, sugar, ginger, cinnamon stick, and lemon juice in a small, heavy-bottom pan. Bring to a boil and boil for 5 minutes.

Stand the pears upright in the pan and cook, turning occasionally, for 15–20 minutes, or until softened. Place each pear on a serving plate.

3 To make the chocolate sauce, place the cream and chocolate in a heatproof bowl and set over a pan of gently simmering water until

the chocolate has melted. Stir until smooth. Transfer to a pitcher and serve immediately with the warm pears.

baked peaches with chocolate

cook: 30 mins   prep: 15 mins   serves 4

This is a delicious variation on the classic Italian pairing of peaches baked with a filling of amaretti cookies.

cook's tip

Choose peaches that are ripe but firm. If they are overripe, they will collapse during cooking. Use a sharp knife to cut the peeled peaches, then carefully prize out and discard the pit, leaving the peach half intact.

INGREDIENTS

2 tbsp unsalted butter, softened, plus
extra for greasing

3 oz/85 g amaretti cookies,
coarsely crushed

1 oz/25 g semisweet chocolate,
finely grated

4 large peaches

1 tbsp golden superfine sugar

crème fraîche or sour cream, to serve

1 Preheat the oven to 375°F/190°C. Grease a shallow baking dish with butter. Place the cookies, grated chocolate, and butter in a bowl and mix together. Place the peaches in a separate heatproof bowl and cover with boiling water. Let stand for 1 minute, then transfer to a bowl of cold water and let stand for an additional minute.

2 Remove the peaches from the water and peel off the skins. Cut each peach in half and remove the pit. Using a teaspoon, scoop out a little flesh from each peach half. Chop the flesh and add to the cookies mixture.

3 Fill each peach half with the amaretti cookie mixture, then sprinkle with sugar. Bake in the oven for 30 minutes, or until the peaches are soft and the filling is crisp. Transfer to a serving plate and serve hot with crème fraîche or sour cream.

exotic fruit chocolate crêpes

serves 4 **prep: 15 mins, plus** ⟲ **20 mins standing** **cook: 15 mins** ⏲

Everybody loves crêpes, and when they are filled with fruit, they are impossible to resist. Dust with confectioners' sugar and eat at once

INGREDIENTS

¾ cup all-purpose flour

2 tbsp unsweetened cocoa

pinch of salt

1 egg, beaten

1¼ cups milk

oil, for frying

confectioners' sugar, for dusting

FILLING

scant ½ cup strained plain yogurt

1⅛ cups mascarpone cheese

confectioners' sugar (optional)

1 mango, peeled and diced

generous 1 cup strawberries, hulled and quartered

2 passion fruit

variation

Other combinations of fruit would also work well, such as mixed summer berries or raspberries, bananas, pears, and apples.

cook's tip

The crêpes can be made in advance, then wrapped in foil and reheated in a warm oven. Make sure the crêpes are thoroughly heated through before filling and serving.

1 To make the filling, place the yogurt and mascarpone cheese in a bowl and sweeten with confectioners' sugar, if you like. Place the mango and strawberries in a bowl and mix together. Cut the passion fruit in half, scoop out the pulp and seeds, and add to the mango and strawberries. Stir together, then set aside.

2 To make the crêpes, sift the flour, unsweetened cocoa, and salt into a bowl and make a well in the center. Add the egg and whisk with a balloon whisk. Gradually beat in the milk, drawing in the flour from the sides, to make a smooth batter. Cover and let stand for 20 minutes. Heat a small amount of oil in a 7-inch/18-cm crêpe pan or skillet. Pour in just enough batter to thinly coat the bottom of the pan. Cook over medium–high heat for 1 minute, then turn and cook the other side for 30–60 seconds, or until cooked through.

3 Transfer the crêpe to a plate and keep hot. Repeat with the remaining batter, stacking the cooked crêpes on top of each other with waxed paper in between. Keep warm in the oven while cooking the remainder. Divide the filling between the crêpes, then roll up and dust with confectioners' sugar. Serve.

chocolate fondue

cook: 5 mins   prep: 20 mins   serves 6

Chilled fresh fruit dipped into a warm chocolate sauce makes a
simple yet sumptuous dessert. It is perfect for entertaining guests.

variation

If serving to children, substitute orange
juice for the brandy. In addition to fruit
for dipping, serve pieces of cake,
cookies, meringues, or marshmallows.

cook's tip

If you do not have a fondue pot,
simply melt the chocolate in a small
pan and transfer to an attractive bowl
for serving. The chocolate will thicken
more quickly than if it is kept warm
over a burner.

INGREDIENTS

1 pineapple	FONDUE
1 mango	9 oz/250 g semisweet chocolate,
12 cape gooseberries	broken into pieces
generous 1 cup fresh strawberries	⅔ cup heavy cream
generous 1½ cups seeded green grapes	2 tbsp brandy

1 Using a sharp knife,
peel and core the
pineapple, then cut the flesh
into cubes. Peel the mango
and cut the flesh into cubes.
Peel back the papery outer
skin of the cape gooseberries
and twist at the top to make a
"handle." Arrange all the fruit
on 6 serving plates and let chill
in the refrigerator.

2 To make the fondue,
place the chocolate and
cream in a fondue pot. Heat
gently, stirring constantly, until
the chocolate has melted. Stir
in the brandy until thoroughly
blended and the chocolate
mixture is smooth.

3 Place the fondue pot
over the burner to keep
warm. To serve, allow each
guest to dip the fruit into the
sauce, using fondue forks or
bamboo skewers.

chocolate fruit crumble

serves 4 **prep: 10 mins** (L) **cook: 40–45 mins** (L)

The addition of chocolate in a crumble topping makes it even more of a treat, and it is also a good way of enticing children to eat a fruit dessert.

INGREDIENTS

6 tbsp butter, plus extra for greasing

14 oz/400 g canned apricots, in natural juice

1 lb/450 g cooking apples, peeled and thickly sliced

scant ⅔ cup all-purpose flour

½ cup rolled oats

4 tbsp superfine sugar

generous ½ cup chocolate chips

---

variation

Other fruits can be used—pears with fresh or frozen raspberries work well. If you do not use canned fruit, add 4 tablespoons of orange juice to the fruit.

1 Preheat the oven to 180°C/350°F. Grease an ovenproof dish with a little butter.

2 Drain the apricots, reserving 4 tablespoons of the juice. Place the apples and apricots in the prepared ovenproof dish with the reserved apricot juice and toss to mix thoroughly.

3 Sift the flour into a large bowl. Cut the butter into small cubes and rub it in with your fingertips until the mixture resembles fine bread crumbs. Stir in the rolled oats, superfine sugar, and chocolate chips.

4 Sprinkle the crumble mixture over the apples and apricots and level the top roughly. Do not press the crumble down onto the fruit. Bake in the preheated oven for 40–45 minutes, or until the topping is golden. Serve the crumble hot or cold.

chocolate eve's pudding

cook: 50 mins   **prep: 15 mins**   **serves 4**

*Eve's Pudding is traditionally made with apples, but here it is
made with fresh raspberries and white chocolate sponge, with
a tasty bitter chocolate sauce.*

variation

Try using semisweet chocolate instead
of white chocolate, and top with
apricot halves, covered with peach
schnapps and apricot conserve.

INGREDIENTS

2 eating apples

8 oz/225 g fresh or frozen raspberries

4 tbsp seedless raspberry jelly

2 tbsp port (optional)

TOPPING

4 tbsp soft margarine

4 tbsp superfine sugar

½ cup self-rising flour, sifted

1¾ oz/50 g white chocolate, grated

1 egg

2 tbsp milk

Chocolate Sauce (see page 13)

1 Preheat the oven to 350°F/180°C. Peel, core, and slice the apples. Place in a shallow 5-cup/ 1.2-liter ovenproof dish with the raspberries.

2 Place the raspberry jelly and port, if using, in a small pan and heat gently until the jelly melts and blends with the port. Pour the mixture over the fruit.

3 Place the margarine, sugar, flour, white chocolate, egg, and milk in a bowl and mix until smooth. Spoon the mixture over the fruit and level the top.

4 Bake in the hot oven for 40–45 minutes, or until the top is springy to the touch. Make the Chocolate Sauce, then serve warm with the pudding.

barbecued chocolate bananas

serves 4　　　　**prep: 5 mins** ↺　　　　**cook: 10 mins** ↺

This is a simple dessert to serve at the end of a barbecue. Open up the foil pockets carefully as they are hot. Serve with cream.

INGREDIENTS

4 bananas

1¾ oz/50 g chocolate chips

1¾ oz/50 g miniature marshmallows

whipped cream, to serve

variation
For a fruitier flavor, add a selection of other fruits to each pocket, such as whole strawberries and raspberries, or peach and mango slices.

1 Using a sharp knife, slit the banana skins and almost through the bananas. Push chocolate chips and marshmallows into the slits, then wrap tightly in foil.

2 Place the banana and chocolate pockets on a grill rack and cook over hot coals on a lit barbecue for 10 minutes, turning after 5 minutes.

3 Open up the pockets carefully and serve the bananas with whipped cream.

cherry & chocolate clafoutis

🕐 cook: 50–60 mins   🕐 prep: 15 mins   serves 6–8

Clafoutis is a traditional dessert from the South of France made with black cherries, and chocolate and Kirsch makes it taste superb.

variation

Other fruit, such as plums or apples, can be used instead of the black cherries, if they are unavailable.

cook's tip

The clafoutis can be served straight from the oven, but it is best if it is left to cool slightly, then served warm with a little cream.

INGREDIENTS

butter, for greasing

3 cups black cherries, pitted

2 tbsp golden granulated sugar

3 eggs

generous ¼ cup golden superfine sugar

½ cup self-rising flour

2 tbsp unsweetened cocoa

⅔ cup cream

1¼ cups milk

2 tbsp Kirsch (optional)

confectioners' sugar, for dusting

fresh whole black cherries, to decorate

cream, to serve

1. Preheat the oven to 375°F/190°C. Grease a 9-inch/23-cm ovenproof pie dish with butter. Arrange the cherries in the dish, sprinkle with the granulated sugar and set aside.

2. Place the eggs and superfine sugar in a bowl and whisk together until light and frothy. Sift the flour and unsweetened cocoa onto a plate and add, all at once, to the egg mixture. Beat in thoroughly, then whisk in the cream, followed by the milk and Kirsch, if using. Pour the batter over the cherries.

3. Bake in the oven for 50–60 minutes, or until slightly risen and set in the center. Dust with confectioners' sugar and decorate with cherries. Serve warm with cream.

chocolate apple pie

⏱ **cook: 40 mins**   ⏱ **prep: 25 mins, plus 30 mins chilling**   **serves 6**

Easy-to-make crumbly chocolate pie dough encases a tasty apple filling studded with chocolate chips—a guaranteed family favorite.

cook's tip

When making dough, use as little cold water as possible to bind the dough because adding too much makes the dough sticky and difficult to handle.

INGREDIENTS

4 tbsp unsweetened cocoa
1 cup all-purpose flour, plus extra for dusting
3½ oz/100 g softened butter
4 tbsp superfine sugar
2 egg yolks
few drops of vanilla extract
1–2 tbsp cold water

FILLING
1 lb 10 oz/750 g cooking apples
2 tbsp butter
½ tsp ground cinnamon
generous ¼ cup semisweet chocolate chips
egg white, beaten
½ tsp superfine sugar, for sprinkling

1 To make the pie dough, sift the cocoa and flour into a large bowl, add the butter and rub it in until the mixture resembles fine bread crumbs. Stir in the sugar. Add the egg yolks, vanilla extract, and enough water to mix to a dough.

2 Roll out the dough on a lightly floured counter and use to line a deep 8-inch/20-cm tart or cake pan. Let chill in the refrigerator for 30 minutes. Roll out any trimmings and cut out some dough leaves to decorate the top of the pie.

3 Preheat the oven to 350°F/180°C. Peel, core, and thickly slice the apples. Place half the apple slices in a heavy-bottom pan with the butter and cinnamon and cook over low heat, stirring occasionally, until the apples soften.

4 Stir in the uncooked apple slices, let cool slightly, then stir in the chocolate chips. Prick the base of the pastry shell and pile the apple mixture into it. Arrange the dough leaves on top. Brush the leaves with a little egg white and sprinkle with superfine sugar.

5 Bake in the preheated oven for 35 minutes, or until the pastry is crisp. Serve warm or cold.

pecan & chocolate pie

⏱ **cook: 40–45 mins**   🕐 **prep: 25 mins**   **serves 6–8**

Pecan pie is an all-time American favorite. Adding chocolate makes it even more luxurious.

variation

Replace the Rich Unsweetened Pie Dough with the Basic Chocolate Pie Dough (see page 13) and serve with crème fraîche instead of cream.

cook's tip

When rolling out pie dough, do not use too much flour, as this changes the texture of the dough, and remember to roll in one direction only. Cover the pie with foil if the dough becomes too brown while baking.

INGREDIENTS

1 quantity of Rich Unsweetened Pie Dough (see page 13)
whipped cream, to serve
ground cinnamon, for dusting

FILLING
2 oz/55 g butter
3 tbsp unsweetened cocoa
1 cup corn syrup
3 eggs
⅜ cup firmly packed dark brown sugar
¾ cup shelled pecans, chopped

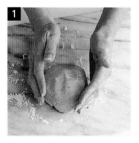

1 Roll out the chilled dough on a lightly floured counter and use to line an 8-inch/20-cm tart pan.

2 Preheat the oven to 375°F/190°C. To make the filling, place the butter in a small, heavy-bottom pan and heat gently until melted. Sift in the cocoa and stir in the syrup.

3 Place the eggs and sugar in a large bowl and beat together. Add the syrup mixture and the chopped pecans and stir. Pour the mixture into the prepared pastry shell.

4 Place the pie on a preheated baking sheet and bake in the preheated oven for 35–40 minutes, or until the filling is just set. Let cool slightly and serve warm with a spoonful of whipped cream, dusted with ground cinnamon.

chocolate bread & butter pudding

serves 6   **prep: 15 mins, plus 10 mins soaking**   **cook: 1 hr**

This traditional nursery pudding is given a brand new twist with semisweet chocolate added to the custard.

INGREDIENTS

2½ cups milk

⅔ cup heavy cream

2¾ oz/75 g semisweet chocolate, broken into pieces

2½ oz/70 g butter, softened, plus extra for greasing

6 thick slices of fruit bread

3 eggs

generous ¼ cup golden superfine sugar

1 tbsp raw brown sugar

1 tsp ground cinnamon

---

variation

Instead of using fruit bread, use white bread and sprinkle some dried fruit in between the slices.

---

cook's tip

This pudding is cooked in a bain-marie, which is a roasting pan filled with water. This helps to slow down the cooking process and prevent the egg custard curdling.

1 Preheat the oven to 350°F/180°C. Lightly grease a 6-cup/1.5-liter shallow ovenproof dish with butter. Place the milk, cream, and chocolate in a large, heavy-bottom pan and heat gently until the chocolate has melted. Butter the slices of bread and cut into triangles. Arrange the bread in the prepared dish.

2 Whisk the eggs and superfine sugar into the chocolate milk and pour over the bread. Let soak for 10 minutes. Gently push the bread down into the custard.

3 Place the raw brown sugar and cinnamon in a small bowl and mix together. Sprinkle over the top of the pudding. Place the dish in a roasting pan and pour in enough hot water to come halfway up the sides of the dish. Bake in the preheated oven for 50–55 minutes, or until the custard is lightly set and the top is golden brown.

chocolate queen of puddings

cook: 40–45 mins   **prep: 25 mins**   **serves 4**

An old time favorite with an up-to-date twist, this pudding makes the perfect end to a special family meal.

variation

If you like, add ⅓ cup dry unsweetened coconut to the bread crumbs and omit the black cherry jelly.

cook's tip

To achieve the best results when making meringue, make sure that all your utensils and bowls are very clean and free from any grease, otherwise the egg whites will not whisk up successfully.

INGREDIENTS

1¾ oz/50 g semisweet chocolate

2 cups chocolate-flavored milk

1¾ cups fresh white or

whole-wheat bread crumbs

scant ⅔ cup superfine sugar

2 eggs, separated

4 tbsp black cherry jelly

1 Preheat the oven to 350°F/180°C. Break the chocolate into small pieces and place in a small, heavy-bottom pan with the chocolate-flavored milk. Heat gently, stirring constantly, until the chocolate melts. Bring almost to a boil, then remove the pan from the heat.

2 Place the bread crumbs in a large bowl with 2 tablespoons of the sugar. Pour over the chocolate milk and mix. Beat in the egg yolks.

3 Spoon the mixture into a 5-cup/1.2-liter pie dish and bake in the preheated oven for 25–30 minutes, or until set and firm to the touch.

4 Whisk the egg whites in a large, spotlessly clean, greasefree bowl until soft peaks form. Gradually whisk in the remaining sugar and whisk until you have a thick, glossy meringue.

5 Spread the black cherry jelly over the surface of the chocolate mixture and pile or pipe the meringue on top. Return to the oven for 15 minutes, or until the meringue is crisp and golden. Serve immediately.

chocolate meringue pie

serves 6   **prep: 25 mins** ⌚   **cook: 35 mins** ⌚

Crumbly cookie base, rich creamy chocolate filling topped with fluffy meringue—what could be more indulgent than this dessert?

INGREDIENTS

8 oz/225 g semisweet chocolate graham crackers

4 tbsp butter

FILLING

3 egg yolks

4 tbsp superfine sugar

4 tbsp cornstarch

2½ cups milk

3½ oz/100 g semisweet chocolate, melted (see pages 9–10)

MERINGUE

2 egg whites

½ cup superfine sugar

¼ tsp vanilla extract

---

variation

Instead of the semisweet chocolate cookies, you can use either gingersnaps or even amaretti cookies.

---

cook's tip

When cooking with chocolate, try to find the chocolate with the highest cocoa butter content as this gives a far superior taste.

1 Preheat the oven to 375°F/160°C. Place the crackers in a plastic bag and crush with a rolling pin, then transfer to a large bowl. Place the butter in a small, heavy-bottom pan and heat gently until just melted, then stir it into the cracker crumbs until well mixed. Press into the bottom and up the sides of a 9-inch/23-cm tart pan or dish.

2 To make the filling, place the egg yolks, superfine sugar, and cornstarch in a large bowl and beat until they form a smooth paste, adding a little of the milk, if necessary. Place the milk into a small, heavy-bottom pan and heat gently until almost boiling, then slowly pour it onto the egg mixture, whisking well.

3 Return the mixture to the pan and cook gently, whisking, until thick. Remove from the heat. Whisk in the melted chocolate, then pour it onto the cracker base.

4 To make the meringue, whisk the egg whites in a large, spotlessly clean, greasefree bowl until soft peaks form. Gradually whisk in two-thirds of the sugar until the mixture is stiff and glossy. Fold in the remaining sugar and vanilla extract.

5 Spread the meringue over the filling, swirling the surface with the back of a spoon to give it an attractive finish. Bake in the center of the oven for 30 minutes, or until golden. Serve hot or just warm.

chocolate cake with rosemary custard

serves 8 | prep: 25 mins, plus 40 mins cooling/infusing | cook: 1 hr 20 mins

This cake is good served cold, but it is even more special when served warm with a delicate rosemary-flavored custard.

INGREDIENTS

4 oz/115 g unsalted butter, plus extra for greasing

5½ oz/150 g semisweet chocolate, broken into pieces

3 large eggs, separated, plus 1 extra egg white

generous ½ cup golden superfine sugar

¾ tsp cream of tartar

2 tbsp all-purpose flour

1 tsp ground cinnamon

3 tbsp ground almonds

confectioners' sugar, for dusting

fresh rosemary sprigs, to decorate

CUSTARD

2 fresh rosemary sprigs

1 vanilla bean split

1¼ cups light cream

⅔ cup milk

5 large egg yolks

3 tbsp golden superfine sugar

variation

As an alternative to rosemary, the custard could be flavored with orange rind, bay leaves, brandy, or a liqueur of your choice.

cook's tip

Use a sharp knife to split the vanilla bean in half lengthwise and use a slotted spoon to remove the bean from the custard before serving.

1 Preheat the oven to 350°F/180°C. Grease and line the bottom of an 8½-inch/22-cm round cake pan. Melt the chocolate and butter in a heatproof bowl and set over a pan of simmering water until melted. Stir in the egg yolks and half the sugar. Place the egg whites and cream of tartar in a clean bowl and beat until soft peaks form. Gradually beat in the remaining sugar until stiff but not dry. Sift the flour and cinnamon into another bowl and stir in the almonds. Fold into the egg white mixture, then fold into the chocolate mixture.

2 Spoon into the cake pan and stand in a roasting pan. Pour in enough hot water to come halfway up the sides of the pan. Bake for 1 hour–1 hour 10 minutes, or until firm to the touch. Remove from the roasting pan, cover, and let stand for 10 minutes before turning out onto a wire rack to cool.

3 Make the custard. Heat the rosemary, vanilla bean, cream, and milk in a pan until almost boiling. Remove from the heat and let infuse for 30 minutes. Beat the egg yolks and sugar together until thick and pale. Reheat the cream mixture, strain onto the egg mixture and whisk in. Set the bowl over a pan of simmering water and stir until thick. Dust the cake with confectioners' sugar, decorate with rosemary, and serve with the custard.

chocolate cranberry sponge

cook: 1 hr 10 mins   **prep: 20 mins**   **serves 4**

The sharpness of the fruit contrasts deliciously with the sweetness
of the chocolate in this wonderful, fluffy sponge pudding.

variation

Serve with Chocolate Sauce (see
page 13) and add 1 tablespoon
of brandy or rum to the chocolate
and cream.

cook's tip

If you don't have a steamer, place
the bowl on a foil sling in a large pan
and fill with enough water to come
halfway up the sides of the bowl.
Cook as in main recipe, then use the
sling to remove the bowl.

INGREDIENTS

4 tbsp unsalted butter, plus
extra for greasing

4 tbsp dark brown sugar, plus
extra for sprinkling

½ cup cranberries, thawed if frozen

1 large cooking apple

2 eggs, lightly beaten

½ cup self-rising flour

3 tbsp unsweetened cocoa

SAUCE

6 oz/175 g semisweet chocolate

1¾ cups evaporated milk

1 tsp vanilla extract

½ tsp almond extract

1 Grease a 5-cup/
1.2-liter ovenproof
bowl with a little butter, then
sprinkle with brown sugar to
coat the sides. Tip out any
excess. Place the cranberries
in a large bowl. Using a sharp
knife, peel, core, and dice
the apple and mix with the
cranberries, then place
the fruit in the prepared
ovenproof bowl.

2 Place the butter, sugar,
and eggs in a large
bowl. Sift in the flour and
cocoa and beat until well
mixed. Pour the mixture on top
of the fruit, then cover with
foil and tie with string. Place
the bowl in a steamer set over
a pan of simmering water and
steam for 1 hour, or until risen,
topping up with boiling water,
as necessary.

3 Meanwhile, make the
sauce. Break the
chocolate into pieces and place
in a heatproof bowl set over a
pan of simmering water with
the milk. Stir constantly, until
the chocolate has melted, then
remove the bowl from the
heat. Whisk in the vanilla and
almond extracts and beat until
thick and smooth.

4 To serve, remove the
pudding and discard the
foil. Run a round-bladed knife
round the side of the bowl,
place a serving plate on top of
the pudding and, holding them
together, invert. Serve
immediately with the sauce.

steamed chocolate pudding

serves 4–6   **prep: 25 mins** ⟲   **cook: 1 hr 40 mins** ⟳

This is as far removed from a school lunch steamed pudding as anything could possibly be! It is best served as soon as it is cooked.

INGREDIENTS

4 oz/115 g butter, softened,
plus extra for greasing

½ cup light brown sugar

2 eggs, beaten

scant ⅔ cup self-rising flour

¼ cup unsweetened cocoa

1–2 tbsp milk (optional)

½ cup semisweet chocolate chips

SAUCE

2 oz/55 g butter

¼ cup light brown sugar

3 tbsp brandy

2 tbsp blanched whole hazelnuts

⅓ cup luxury mixed dried fruit

cook's tip

You can make the pudding in advance. Place the covered bowl back into a pan of boiling water, on a trivet, for 20–30 minutes before serving.

1 Grease a 5-cup/ 1.2-liter ovenproof bowl and line the base with a small circle of waxed paper. Beat the butter and sugar together until light and fluffy. Gradually beat in the eggs. Sift the flour and cocoa into the mixture and fold in. Add a little milk, if necessary, to make a dropping consistency. Stir in the chocolate chips.

2 Spoon the mixture into the prepared bowl. Cut out a circle of waxed paper and a circle of foil, both about 3 inches/7.5 cm larger than the top of the bowl. Place the paper on top of the foil and grease the upper surface. Make a fold in the center of both, then use to cover the bowl, paper-side down, and secure with string. Place the

bowl on a trivet in a pan and pour in enough boiling water to come halfway up the sides of the bowl. Cover and let simmer for 1½ hours, topping up with extra boiling water as necessary.

3 To make the sauce, place the butter and sugar in a small pan and heat gently until the sugar has

dissolved and the mixture looks slightly caramelized. Add the brandy and let bubble for 1 minute. Stir in the hazelnuts and dried fruit. Carefully turn the pudding out onto a plate and spoon the sauce over. Serve immediately.

individual chocolate fondant puddings

cook: 20 mins   **prep: 15 mins**   **serves 4**

As you cut into these tasty puddings, you will discover their seductive warm liquid chocolate centers.

variation

For a truly tempting presentation, you can also serve these puddings with a raspberry coulis and a few fresh raspberries on the side.

INGREDIENTS

3½ oz/100 g butter,
plus extra for greasing
½ cup golden superfine sugar,
plus extra for coating
3½ oz/100 g semisweet chocolate,
broken into pieces
2 large eggs
1 tsp vanilla extract
2 tbsp all-purpose flour
confectioners' sugar, for dusting
vanilla ice cream, to serve

1 Preheat the oven to 400°F/200°C. Grease 4 x ¾-cup/175-ml ovenproof bowls or ramekins and coat with superfine sugar. Place the butter and chocolate in a heatproof bowl and set over a pan of gently simmering water until melted. Stir until smooth. Let cool.

2 Place the eggs, vanilla extract, superfine sugar, and flour in a bowl and whisk together. Stir in the melted chocolate. Pour the mixture into the prepared molds and place on a baking sheet. Bake in the oven for 12–15 minutes, or until the puddings are well risen and set on the outside but still melting inside.

3 Let stand for 1 minute, then turn the puddings out onto 4 serving plates. Dust with confectioners' sugar and serve immediately with vanilla ice cream.

saucy chocolate pudding

serves 4–6   **prep: 10 mins**   **cook: 50–60 mins**

When you first remove this pudding from the oven, it doesn't look particularly impressive. However, when you cut into it, you find a lovely pool of chocolate sauce at the bottom of the dish.

INGREDIENTS

3 oz/85 g butter, softened,
plus extra for greasing

scant ½ cup self-rising flour

¼ cup unsweetened cocoa

1 tsp ground cinnamon

generous ½ cup golden superfine sugar

1 egg

2 tbsp dark brown sugar

¼ cup shelled pecans, chopped

1¼ cups hot black coffee

confectioners' sugar, for dusting

whipped cream, to serve

---

cook's tip

Take care not to open the oven for the first 40 minutes of the cooking time, otherwise the pudding may sink quite considerably.

1 Preheat the oven to 325°F/160°C. Grease a shallow 5-cup/1.2-liter ovenproof dish with a little butter. Sift the flour, unsweetened cocoa, and cinnamon into a large bowl. Add the butter, ⅜ cup of the superfine sugar, and the egg and beat together until the mixture is well blended. Turn into the prepared dish and sprinkle with the light brown sugar and the pecans.

2 Pour the coffee into a large pitcher, stir in the remaining superfine sugar until dissolved and carefully pour over the pudding.

3 Bake in the oven for 50–60 minutes, or until firm to the touch in the center. Dust with a little confectioners' sugar and serve with whipped cream.

cappuccino soufflé puddings

cook: 20 mins   **prep: 25 mins**   **serves 6**

*These light and airy puddings simply melt in the mouth.
Served with vanilla ice cream, they will provide the perfect
finale to any meal.*

variation

Kahlua is a liqueur with a distinctive coffee flavor, but if you cannot find it, substitute rum or brandy as an alternative flavoring.

INGREDIENTS

butter, for greasing

2 tbsp golden superfine sugar, plus extra for coating

6 tbsp whipping cream

2 tsp instant espresso coffee granules

2 tbsp Kahlua

3 large eggs, separated, plus 1 extra egg white

5½ oz/150 g semisweet chocolate, melted and cooled (see pages 9–10)

unsweetened cocoa, for dusting

vanilla ice cream, to serve

1 Preheat the oven to 375°F/190°C. Lightly grease the sides of 6 x ¾-cup/175-ml ramekins with butter and coat with superfine sugar. Place the ramekins on a baking sheet.

2 Place the cream in a small, heavy-bottom pan and heat gently. Stir in the coffee until it has dissolved, then stir in the Kahlua. Divide the coffee mixture between the prepared ramekins.

3 Place the egg whites in a clean, greasefree bowl and whisk until soft peaks form, then gradually whisk in the sugar until stiff but not dry. Stir the egg yolks and melted chocolate together in a separate bowl, then stir in a little of the whisked egg whites. Gradually fold in the remaining egg whites.

4 Divide the mixture between the dishes. Bake in the preheated oven for 15 minutes, or until just set. Dust with unsweetened cocoa and serve immediately with vanilla ice cream.

hot chocolate soufflé with coffee sabayon

🕙 cook: 50 mins   🕙 prep: 25 mins   serves 4–6

Soufflés, especially chocolate ones, are not as tricky to make as is often thought. The crucial point is to make sure that everyone is sitting at the table when it is ready.

variation

Replace the semisweet chocolate in the soufflé with white chocolate and serve with Chocolate Sauce (see page 13) instead of the sabayon.

cook's tip

A prepared soufflé will keep in the refrigerator for up to 2 hours before cooking and will then still rise.

INGREDIENTS

butter, for greasing

generous ¼ cup golden superfine sugar, plus extra for coating

3 tbsp cornstarch

1⅓ cups milk

4 oz/115 g semisweet chocolate, broken into pieces

4 eggs, separated

confectioners' sugar, for dusting

SABAYON

2 eggs

3 egg yolks

⅜ cup golden superfine sugar

4 tsp instant coffee granules

2 tbsp brandy

1 Preheat the oven to 375°F/190°C. Grease a 4-cup/1-liter soufflé dish with butter and coat with superfine sugar. To make the soufflé, place the cornstarch in a bowl. Add a little milk and stir until smooth. Pour the remaining milk into a heavy-bottom pan and add the chocolate. Heat gently until the chocolate has melted, then stir. Pour the chocolate milk onto the cornstarch paste, stirring. Return to the pan and bring to a boil, stirring. Let simmer for 1 minute. Remove from the heat and stir in the egg yolks, one at a time, and the sugar. Cover and let cool slightly.

2 Place the egg whites in a large, spotlessly clean, greasefree bowl and whisk until starting to stand in soft peaks. Gradually whisk in the superfine sugar until stiff but not dry. Stir a little of the meringue into the chocolate mixture, then carefully fold in the remainder. Pour into the prepared soufflé dish and bake in the preheated oven for 40 minutes, or until it is well risen and wobbles slightly when pushed.

3 Just before the soufflé is ready, make the coffee sabayon. Place all the ingredients in a heavy-bottom pan. Place the pan over very low heat and whisk constantly, until the mixture is thick and light. Dust a little confectioners' sugar over the soufflé and serve immediately, with the sabayon.

hot chocolate cheesecake

serves 8–10 **prep: 25 mins, plus 10 mins chilling** **cook: 1 hr 30 mins**

This decadent cheesecake is doubly chocolatey, with chocolate in the pie dough and the filling. It is delicious served warm.

INGREDIENTS

butter, for greasing

PIE DOUGH
generous 1 cup all-purpose flour
2 tbsp unsweetened cocoa
2¾ oz/75 g butter, diced
2 tbsp golden superfine sugar
¼ cup ground almonds
1 egg yolk

FILLING
2 eggs, separated
scant ⅜ cup golden superfine sugar
1½ cups cream cheese
⅜ cup ground almonds
⅔ cup heavy cream
¼ cup unsweetened cocoa, sifted
1 tsp vanilla extract
confectioners' sugar, for dusting

variation

If you like, make a little extra pie dough and use to form a lattice design on top of the filling, then bake as in main recipe.

cook's tip

To remove the cheesecake easily from the cake pan, stand the pan on top of a can and gently ease the sides down to the counter, leaving the cheesecake on top of the can.

1 Preheat the oven to 325°F/160°C. Grease an 8-inch/20-cm loose-bottom cake pan with butter. To make the pie dough, sift the flour and unsweetened cocoa into a bowl. Add the butter and rub it in until the mixture resembles fine bread crumbs. Stir in the sugar and almonds. Add the egg yolk and enough water to make a soft dough.

Roll out on a lightly floured counter and use to line the pan. Let chill in the refrigerator while preparing the filling.

2 To make the filling, place the egg yolks and superfine sugar in a large bowl and whisk together until thick and pale. Whisk in the cheese, almonds, cream, cocoa, and vanilla extract until blended.

3 Place the egg whites in a clean, greasefree bowl and whisk until stiff but not dry. Stir a little of the whisked egg whites into the cheese mixture, then fold in the remainder. Pour into the pastry shell. Bake in the oven for 1½ hours, or until risen and just firm to the touch. Remove from the pan and dust with confectioners' sugar.

chocolate zabaglione

cook: 5 mins   prep: 10 mins   serves 4

As this recipe only uses a little chocolate, choose one with
a minimum of 70 percent cocoa solids for a good flavor.

variation

For a change, substitute the Marsala wine for dry sherry or brandy and serve with ladyfingers instead of the amaretti cookies.

cook's tip

Make the dessert just before serving as it will separate if left to stand. If it starts to curdle, remove it from the heat and place it in a bowl of cold water. Whisk furiously until the mixture comes together.

INGREDIENTS

4 egg yolks

4 tbsp superfine sugar

1¾ oz/50 g semisweet chocolate

½ cup Marsala wine

unsweetened cocoa, for dusting

amaretti cookies, to serve

1 Place the egg yolks and superfine sugar in a large glass bowl and, using an electric whisk, whisk together until the mixture is very pale.

2 Grate the chocolate finely and, using a spatula, fold into the egg mixture. Fold the Marsala wine into the chocolate mixture.

3 Place the bowl over a pan of gently simmering water and set the electric whisk on the lowest speed or swap to a balloon whisk. Cook gently, whisking constantly, until the mixture thickens. Do not overcook or the mixture will curdle.

4 Spoon the hot mixture into 4 warmed glass dishes or coffee cups and dust with cocoa. Serve as soon as possible, while it is warm, light, and fluffy, with amaretti cookies.

gâteaux, cakes & tarts

*Whether you are baking for a special occasion or just for family or friends, you can
never fail to impress and satisfy with a chocolate cake or tart—it's practically everyone's favorite!
So it's reassuring to know that you don't have to be an experienced or
skillful cook to be able to produce such a crowd-pleaser whenever the fancy
takes you or the need arises.*

*In this section, there are glorious gâteaux, such as Strawberry Chocolate Gâteau
(see page 113) or Chocolate Truffle Torte (see page 115), which can be served as a dessert
or for a celebration, or simpler family favorites, like Banana & Chocolate Teabread (see
page 144) or Chocolate & Vanilla Marble Cake (see page 134). Also featured are some classic
cakes from round the world, including Sicilian Cassata (see page 147) and the Viennese
Sachertorte (see page 128), as well as delicious chocolate tarts, such as Chocolate Fudge Tart
(see page 153) or tangy Lemon & Chocolate Tart (see page 150).*

*Whether your preference is for rich and creamy confections or plainer cakes with no more
than a dusting of unsweetened cocoa for decoration, there is something here to appeal to all
tastes. One thing is for sure—whenever you have a chocolate cake nestling in the cake pan,
it won't be there for long!*

double chocolate roulade

serves 8 **prep: 30 mins, plus 10 hrs standing/chilling** **cook: 20–25 mins**

*A dark chocolate mousse is rolled round white chocolate cream to
make a luscious dessert. Delicious served with summer berries.*

INGREDIENTS

4 eggs, separated

generous ½ cup golden superfine sugar

4 oz/115 g semisweet chocolate,
melted and cooled (see pages 9–10)

1 tsp instant coffee granules, dissolved
in 2 tbsp hot water, cooled

confectioners' sugar, to decorate

unsweetened cocoa, for dusting

fresh raspberries, to serve

FILLING

generous 1 cup whipping cream

5 oz/140 g white chocolate,
broken into pieces

3 tbsp Tia Maria

variation

If you like, substitute the Tia Maria
with the same amount of brandy,
rum, or orange juice.

cook's tip

If you do not have time, it is not
essential to chill the roulade for
2 hours before serving. However,
the roulade firms up in this time and
becomes easier to slice.

1 Preheat the oven to 350°F/180°C. Line a 9 x 13-inch/23 x 33-cm jelly roll pan with nonstick parchment paper. Whisk the egg yolks and sugar in a bowl until pale and mousse-like. Fold in the chocolate, then the coffee. Place the egg whites in a clean bowl and whisk until stiff but not dry. Stir a little of the egg whites into the chocolate mixture, then fold in the remainder. Pour into the pan and bake for 15–20 minutes, or until firm. Cover with a damp dish towel and let stand in the pan for 8 hours, or overnight.

2 Meanwhile, make the filling. Heat the cream until almost boiling. Place the chocolate in a food processor and chop coarsely. With the motor running, pour the cream through the feed tube. Process until smooth. Stir in the Tia Maria. Transfer to a bowl and let cool. Let chill for 8 hours, or overnight.

3 To assemble the roulade, whip the chocolate cream until soft peaks form. Cut a sheet of waxed paper larger than the roulade, place on a counter and sift confectioners' sugar over. Turn the roulade out onto the paper. Peel away the lining paper. Spread the chocolate cream over the roulade and roll up from the short side nearest to you. Transfer to a dish, seam-side down. Let chill for 2 hours, then dust with cocoa. Serve with raspberries.

raspberry dessert cake

serves 8–10 **prep: 20 mins, plus** ⏱ **15 mins cooling** **cook: 40–50 mins** ⏱

The raspberries in this luxurious dark chocolate cake give it a fresh tangy flavor. Serve with fresh raspberries and whipped cream.

INGREDIENTS

8 oz/225 g butter, plus extra
for greasing

9 oz/250 g semisweet chocolate,
broken into pieces

1 tbsp strong dark coffee

5 eggs

⅝ cup golden superfine sugar

¾ cup all-purpose flour

1 tsp ground cinnamon

¾ cup fresh raspberries

confectioners' sugar, for dusting

TO SERVE

fresh raspberries

whipped cream

variation

If fresh raspberries are not available, frozen raspberries may be used. Since these will be softer than fresh fruit, take care to thaw them thoroughly and drain off any excess juice.

1 Preheat the oven to 325°F/160°C. Grease a 9-inch/23-cm cake pan with butter and line the bottom with parchment paper. Place the chocolate, butter, and coffee in a small heatproof bowl and set over a pan of gently simmering water until melted. Stir and let cool slightly.

2 Place the eggs and sugar in a separate bowl and beat together until thick and pale. Gently fold in the chocolate cake batter. Sift the flour and ground cinnamon into a separate bowl, then fold into the chocolate cake batter. Pour into the pan and sprinkle the raspberries evenly over the top.

3 Bake in the oven for 35–45 minutes, or until the cake is well risen and springy to the touch. Let cool in the pan for 15 minutes before turning out onto a large serving plate. Dust with confectioners' sugar before serving with fresh raspberries and cream.

chocolate & mango layer

cook: 1 hr 10 mins   **prep: 30 mins, plus 1 hr cooling**   **serves 12**

Canned peaches can be used instead of mangoes for this deliciously moist cake, if you prefer.

cook's tip

It is very important that the cream is only lightly whipped as it thickens when the cooled chocolate is added. Use a rubber spatula to fold the chocolate in gently.

INGREDIENTS

butter, for greasing

½ cup unsweetened cocoa

⅔ cup boiling water

6 large eggs

scant 1¾ cups superfine sugar

scant 2 cups self-rising flour

1 lb 12 oz/800 g canned mangoes

1 tsp cornstarch

scant 2 cups heavy cream

2¾ oz/75 g semisweet chocolate, grated

1 Preheat the oven to 325°F/160°C. Grease and line a deep 9-inch/23-cm round cake pan. Place the cocoa in a small, heatproof bowl, gradually add the boiling water and blend until smooth.

2 Whisk the eggs and superfine sugar together until light and foamy and the whisk leaves a trail that lasts a few seconds when lifted. Fold in the cocoa mixture. Sift the flour and fold into the cake batter, then pour into the pan and level the top. Bake in the hot oven for 1 hour, or until springy to the touch. Let cool in the pan for 5 minutes, then turn out onto a wire rack and let cool completely. Peel off the paper and cut the cake into 3 layers.

3 Drain the mangoes, reserving the juice. Place one-quarter of them in a blender and purée until smooth. Mix the cornstarch with 3 tablespoons of the juice to form a paste, then add to the mango purée. Transfer to a pan and heat, stirring, until thick. Let cool. Chop the remaining mango. Whip the cream and reserve one-quarter.

Fold the mango into the remaining cream and use to sandwich the layers of cake together. Place on a serving plate. Spread some of the remaining cream round the side of the cake, then press the grated chocolate into the cream. Spread the mango purée over the center and pipe cream rosettes round the top.

strawberry chocolate gâteau

cook: 30–40 mins

prep: 25 mins, plus 30 mins cooling

serves 8

Fresh strawberries and whipped cream with light chocolate sponge make the perfect treat for a hot summer's day.

variation

If you like, replace the Kirsch with another liqueur, such as Cointreau, or use brandy instead.

cook's tip

If you do not want to make the Chocolate Curls, either use the ready-made variety or decorate the side of the cake with crushed chocolate flake bars.

INGREDIENTS

butter, for greasing

SPONGE

3 eggs

generous ½ cup golden superfine sugar

⅔ cup self-rising flour

2 tbsp unsweetened cocoa

FILLING AND TOPPING

generous 1 cup strawberries

1¼ cups heavy cream

½ tsp vanilla extract

1 tbsp confectioners' sugar

2 tbsp Kirsch

Chocolate Curls (see page 10)

1 Preheat the oven to 375°F/190°C. Grease and line an 8½-inch/22-cm cake pan. To make the sponge, place the eggs and sugar in a bowl and whisk until thick and mousse-like, and a trail is left when the whisk is lifted. Sift the flour and unsweetened cocoa into a separate bowl, then fold into the whisked cake batter. Turn into the pan and bake in the oven for 30–40 minutes, or until the cake springs back when pressed in the center. Let stand the pan for 5 minutes, then let cool on a wire rack.

2 Meanwhile, prepare the filling. Set aside 4 strawberries, and hull and slice the remainder. Whip the cream, vanilla extract, and confectioners' sugar together until thick. Set aside two-thirds of the cream and fold the strawberries into the remainder.

3 Slice the sponge horizontally into 2 layers and sprinkle each layer with 1 tablespoon of Kirsch. Place one layer on a plate and spread over the strawberry cream. Place the other sponge layer on top. Place some of the reserved cream in a pastry bag fitted with a fluted tip and spread the remainder over the top and sides of the cake. Coat the sides with Chocolate Curls. Pipe the cream round the top of the cake. Cut the reserved strawberries in half, keeping the stalks intact, and arrange on the piped cream.

orange mousse cake

serves 12　　　**prep: 20 mins, plus 1 hr ⟳ 30 mins cooling/chilling**　　　**cook: 40 mins ⟳**

With a dark chocolate sponge sandwiched together with a light, creamy orange mousse, this spectacular cake is irresistible

INGREDIENTS

6 oz/175 g butter

scant 1 cup superfine sugar

4 eggs, lightly beaten

1 tbsp unsweetened cocoa

generous 1¼ cups self-rising flour

50 g/1¾ oz orange-flavored chocolate

MOUSSE

2 eggs, separated

4 tbsp superfine sugar

scant 1 cup orange juice

2 tsp gelatin

1¼ cups heavy cream

peeled orange slices, to decorate

cook's tip

For best results and a real orange taste, use plain orange-flavored chocolate for the sponge and freshly squeezed orange juice in the mousse.

1 Preheat the oven to 350°F/180°C. Grease and line the bottom of an 8-inch/20-cm springform cake pan. Beat the butter and sugar in a bowl until light and fluffy. Gradually add the eggs, beating well after each addition. Sift the cocoa and flour together and fold into the cake batter. Fold in the orange-flavored chocolate.

2 Pour into the pan and level the top. Bake for 40 minutes, or until springy to the touch. Let stand in the pan for 5 minutes, then turn out and cool on a wire rack. Cut the cold cake into 2 layers.

3 To make the mousse. Beat the egg yolks and sugar together until light, then whisk in the orange juice. Place 3 tablespoons of cold water in a bowl and sprinkle the gelatin over the top. Let stand for 5 minutes, or until spongy, then place over a pan of hot water and stir until dissolved. Stir into the mousse.

4 Whip the cream until just holding its shape, set aside a little for decoration and fold the rest into the mousse. Whisk the egg whites in a clean bowl until soft peaks form, then fold into the mousse. Let stand in a cool place until starting to set, stirring occasionally. Place half the cake in the pan. Pour in the mousse and press the second cake layer on top. Chill until set. Transfer to a dish, pipe cream rosettes on top and lay orange slices in the center.

chocolate truffle torte

cook: 7–10 mins   **prep: 40 mins, plus 4–5 hrs chilling**   **serves 10**

Chocolate and cream on a thin sponge base make this a wickedly rich dessert for an extra special occasion.

cook's tip

It is very important that the cream is only lightly whipped as it thickens when the cooled chocolate is added. Use a rubber spatula to fold the chocolate in gently.

INGREDIENTS

butter, for greasing

generous ¼ cup golden superfine sugar

2 eggs

scant ¼ cup all-purpose flour

¼ cup unsweetened cocoa, plus extra to decorate

¼ cup cold strong black coffee

2 tbsp brandy

TOPPING

2½ cups whipping cream

15 oz/425 g semisweet chocolate, melted and cooled (see pages 9–10)

confectioners' sugar, to decorate

1 Preheat the oven to 425°F/220°C. Grease a 9-inch/23-cm springform cake pan with butter and line the bottom with parchment paper. Place the sugar and eggs in a heatproof bowl and set over a pan of hot water. Whisk together until pale and mousse-like. Sift the flour and unsweetened cocoa into a separate bowl, then fold gently into the cake batter. Pour into the prepared pan and bake in the oven for 7–10 minutes, or until risen and firm to the touch.

2 Transfer to a wire rack to cool. Wash and dry the pan and replace the cooled cake in the pan. Mix the coffee and brandy together and brush over the cake. To make the topping, place the cream in a bowl and whip until very soft peaks form. Carefully fold in the cooled chocolate. Pour the chocolate mixture over the sponge. Let chill in the refrigerator for 4–5 hours, or until set.

3 To decorate the torte, sift unsweetened cocoa over the top and remove carefully from the pan. Using strips of card or waxed paper, sift bands of confectioners' sugar over the torte to create a striped pattern. To serve, cut into slices with a hot knife.

mocha layer cake

serves 8   **prep: 20 mins, plus 30 mins cooling**   **cook: 35–45 mins**

Chocolate cake and a creamy coffee-flavored filling are combined in this delicious mocha cake. Serve with afternoon tea.

INGREDIENTS

butter for greasing

generous 1¼ cups self-rising flour

¼ tsp baking powder

4 tbsp unsweetened cocoa

½ cup superfine sugar

2 eggs

2 tbsp corn syrup

⅔ cup corn oil

⅔ cup milk

FILLING

1 tsp instant coffee

1 tbsp boiling water

1¼ cups heavy cream

2 tbsp confectioners' sugar

TO DECORATE

1¾ oz/50 g semisweet chocolate, grated

Chocolate Caraque (see page 10)

confectioners' sugar, for dusting

variation

Replace the grated chocolate with chopped nuts or flock chocolate. Alternatively arrange Chocolate Leaves round the edge (see page 11).

cook's tip

To test that the cake is cooked, lightly press the center with your fingertips—if it springs back, then it is done. Remove from the oven and let cool in the pan for 5 minutes, then let cool completely on a wire rack.

1 Preheat the oven to 350°F/180°C. Lightly grease 3 x 7-inch/18-cm cake pans.

2 Sift the flour, baking powder, and cocoa into a large bowl, then stir in the sugar. Make a well in the center and stir in the eggs, syrup, corn oil, and milk. Beat with a wooden spoon, gradually mixing in the dry ingredients to make a smooth batter. Divide the mixture between the pans.

3 Bake in the preheated oven for 35–45 minutes, or until springy to the touch. Let stand in the pans for 5 minutes, then turn out and let cool completely on a wire rack.

4 To make the filling, dissolve the instant coffee in the boiling water and place in a large bowl with the cream and confectioners' sugar. Whip until the cream is just holding its shape, then use half the cream to sandwich the 3 cakes together. Spread the remaining cream over the top and sides of the cake. Press the grated chocolate into the cream round the edge of the cake. Transfer the cake to a serving plate. Lay the Chocolate Caraque over the top of the cake. Cut a few thin strips of parchment paper and place on top of the Chocolate Caraque. Dust lightly with confectioners' sugar, then carefully remove the paper. Serve.

double chocolate gâteau

 cook: 55–65 mins   prep: 1 hr,   serves 10
                           plus 2 hrs chilling

This chocolate sponge layered with white chocolate cream and covered in dark chocolate frosting could be served either as a celebration cake or a dessert.

variation

Mix ½ cup fresh raspberries to the whipped cream and use to fill the gâteau. Omit the chocolate, if you like and serve with raspberries.

cook's tip

It is important to use the correct cake pan as it will affect the baking time and the finished cake, so always use the type that is specified in the recipe.

INGREDIENTS

butter, for greasing

FILLING

generous 1 cup whipping cream

8 oz/225 g white chocolate, broken into pieces

SPONGE

8 oz/225 g butter, softened

generous 1 cup golden superfine sugar

4 eggs, beaten

generous 1 cup self-rising flour

½ cup unsweetened cocoa

1–2 tbsp milk (optional)

FROSTING

12 oz/350 g semisweet chocolate, broken into pieces

4 oz/115 g butter

⅓ cup heavy cream

TO DECORATE

Chocolate Curls (see page 10), chilled

4 oz/115 g semisweet chocolate, broken into pieces

2 tsp confectioners' sugar and unsweetened cocoa, mixed together

1 Grease and line the bottom of an 8-inch/20-cm deep round cake pan. To make the filling, heat the cream to almost boiling. Place the white chocolate in a food processor and chop coarsely. With the motor running, pour the cream through the feed tube. Process for 10–15 seconds, or until the mixture is smooth. Transfer to a bowl and let cool. Cover and let chill for 2 hours, or until firm. Whisk until just starting to hold soft peaks.

2 Preheat the oven to 350°F/180°C. To make the sponge, beat the butter and sugar together until light and fluffy. Gradually beat in the eggs. Sift the flour and cocoa into another bowl, then fold into the batter, adding a little milk, if necessary, to make a dropping consistency. Spoon into the pan, level the surface, and bake in the oven for 45–50 minutes, or until springy to the touch and the tip of a knife inserted into the center comes out clean. Let stand in the pan for 5 minutes, then let cool on a wire rack.

3 To make the frosting, melt the chocolate (see pages 9–10). Stir in the butter and cream. Let cool, stirring frequently, until the mixture is a spreading consistency. Slice the cake into 3 layers. Sandwich the layers together with the filling. Cover the cake with frosting, put Chocolate Curls on top, and sift confectioners' sugar and cocoa over the cake.

dark & white chocolate torte

serves 6 **prep: 20 mins, plus 1 hr 20 mins cooling/setting** **cook: 35–40 mins**

If you can't decide if you prefer semisweet chocolate or rich creamy white chocolate then this gâteau is for you

INGREDIENTS

4 eggs

½ cup superfine sugar

¾ cup all-purpose flour

FILLING

1¼ cups heavy cream

5½ oz/150 g semisweet chocolate, broken into small pieces

TOPPING

2¾ oz/75 g white chocolate

1 tbsp butter

1 tbsp milk

4 tbsp confectioners' sugar

cook's tip

Add the finishing touch to this wonderful gâteau by decorating it with Chocolate Caraque (see page 10). Use semisweet or white chocolate for the curls or a mixture of both.

1 Preheat the oven to 350°F/180°C. Grease and line the bottom of an 8-inch/20-cm round springform cake pan. Whisk the eggs and superfine sugar in a large bowl with an electric whisk for 10 minutes, or until the mixture is very light and foamy and the whisk leaves a trail that lasts a few seconds when lifted.

2 Sift the flour and fold in with a metal spoon or spatula. Pour into the prepared pan and bake in the oven for 35–40 minutes, or until springy to the touch. Let cool slightly, then transfer to a wire rack to cool completely.

3 For the filling, place the cream in a pan and bring to a boil, stirring. Add the chocolate and stir until melted. Remove from the heat, transfer to a bowl, and let cool. Beat with a wooden spoon until thick.

4 Slice the cold cake horizontally into 2 layers. Sandwich the layers together with the semisweet chocolate cream and place on a wire rack.

5 For the topping, melt the chocolate and butter together and stir until blended. Whisk in the milk and confectioners' sugar. Continue whisking for a few minutes until the frosting is cool. Pour it over the cake and spread with a spatula to coat the top and sides. Let set.

devil's food cake

cook: 30 mins

prep: 20 mins, plus 1 hr cooling

serves 10–12

This is an American classic, consisting of a rich, melt-in-the-mouth chocolate cake that has a delicious citrus-flavored frosting.

variation

For a touch of decadence, replace the citrus-flavored frosting with a Chocolate Fudge Frosting (see page 122) and serve with fresh berries.

INGREDIENTS

8 oz/225 g butter, plus extra for greasing

3½ oz/100 g semisweet chocolate

generous 1⅛ cups self-rising flour

1 tsp baking soda

2 cups firmly packed dark brown sugar

1 tsp vanilla extract

3 eggs

½ cup buttermilk

FROSTING

1½ cups superfine sugar

2 egg whites

1 tbsp lemon juice

3 tbsp orange juice

candied orange peel, to decorate

1. Preheat the oven to 375°F/190°C. Lightly grease and line the bottoms of 2 x 8-inch/20-cm shallow round cake pans. Melt the chocolate (see pages 9–10). Sift the flour and baking soda together.

2. Place the butter and sugar in a large bowl and beat until pale and fluffy.

Beat in the vanilla extract and the eggs, one at a time, beating well after each addition. Add a little flour if the mixture starts to curdle.

3. Fold the melted chocolate into the mixture until well blended. Fold in the remaining flour, then stir in the buttermilk and 1 cup boiling water.

4. Divide the mixture between the pans and level the tops. Bake in the hot oven for 30 minutes, or until springy to the touch. Let cool in the pan for 5 minutes, then transfer to a wire rack and let cool completely.

5. Place the frosting ingredients in a large bowl set over a pan of simmering water. Using an electric whisk, whisk until thick and forming soft peaks. Remove from the heat and whisk until the mixture is cool.

6. Sandwich the 2 cakes together with a little of the frosting, then spread the remainder over the sides and top of the cake. Decorate with candied orange peel.

chocolate fudge cake

serves 8   **prep: 25 mins, plus ⟳ 2 hrs cooling/chilling**   **cook: 35–45 mins ⟳**

This rich chocolate cake with a rich, soft fudgy frosting makes the perfect birthday cake for a chocolate-lover.

INGREDIENTS

6 oz/175 g unsalted butter, softened, plus extra for greasing

generous 1 cup golden superfine sugar

3 eggs, beaten

3 tbsp corn syrup

3 tbsp ground almonds

generous 1 cup self-rising flour

pinch of salt

¼ cup unsweetened cocoa

FROSTING

8 oz/225 g semisweet chocolate, broken into pieces

¼ cup dark brown sugar

8 oz/225 g unsalted butter, diced

5 tbsp evaporated milk

½ tsp vanilla extract

variation

To make the frosting really creamy, substitute the evaporated milk with the same amount of light cream.

cook's tip

Beat the eggs into the butter and sugar one at a time, and beat well after each addition. If the cake batter starts to curdle while you are adding the eggs, beat in a little of the flour.

1 Grease and line the bottom of 2 x 8-inch/20-cm cake pans. To make the frosting, place the chocolate, sugar, butter, evaporated milk, and vanilla extract in a heavy-bottom pan. Heat gently, stirring constantly, until melted. Pour into a bowl and let cool. Cover and let chill in the refrigerator for 1 hour, or until spreadable.

2 Preheat the oven to 350°F/180°C. Place the butter and sugar in a bowl and beat together until light and fluffy. Gradually beat in the eggs. Stir in the syrup and ground almonds. Sift the flour, salt, and unsweetened cocoa into a separate bowl, then fold into the cake batter. Add a little water, if necessary, to make a dropping consistency.

Spoon the cake batter into the prepared pans and bake in the oven for 30–35 minutes, or until springy to the touch and the tip of a knife inserted in the center comes out clean.

3 Let stand in the pans for 5 minutes, then turn out onto wire racks to cool completely. When the cakes are cold, sandwich them

together with half the frosting. Spread the remaining frosting over the top and sides of the cake, swirling it to give a frosted appearance.

chocolate cake with coffee syrup

🌡 **cook: 50 mins**   🕐 **prep: 15 mins**   **serves 12**

An intensely flavored chocolate cake that is particularly good served slightly warm, with sour cream, as a dessert.

variation

Split the cake in half horizontally and fill the center with whipped cream and pitted Morello cherries, then serve with the coffee syrup.

cook's tip

When making syrups, keep a pastry brush and a pitcher of cold water nearby to brush the sides of the pan occasionally with water. This helps to prevent crystallization.

INGREDIENTS

4 oz/115 g unsalted butter, plus extra for greasing

8 oz/225 g semisweet chocolate, broken into pieces

1 tbsp strong black coffee

4 large eggs

2 egg yolks

generous ½ cup golden superfine sugar

generous ⅓ cup all-purpose flour

2 tsp ground cinnamon

scant ½ cup ground almonds

chocolate-covered coffee beans, to decorate

SYRUP

1¼ cups strong black coffee

generous ½ cup golden superfine sugar

1 cinnamon stick

1 Preheat the oven to 375°F/190°C. Grease and line the bottom of a deep 8-inch/20-cm round cake pan. Place the chocolate, butter, and coffee in a heatproof bowl and set over a pan of gently simmering water until melted. Stir to blend, then remove from the heat and let cool slightly.

2 Place the whole eggs, egg yolks, and sugar in a separate bowl and whisk together until thick and pale. Sift the flour and cinnamon over the egg mixture. Add the almonds and the chocolate mixture and fold in carefully. Spoon the cake batter into the prepared pan. Bake in the oven for 35 minutes, or until the tip of a knife inserted into the center comes out clean. Let cool slightly before turning out onto a serving plate.

3 Meanwhile, make the syrup. Place the coffee, sugar, and cinnamon stick in a heavy-bottom pan and heat gently, stirring, until the sugar has dissolved. Increase the heat and boil for 5 minutes, or until reduced and thickened slightly. Keep warm. Pierce the surface of the cake with a toothpick, then drizzle over half the coffee syrup. Decorate with chocolate-covered coffee beans and serve, cut into wedges, with the remaining coffee syrup.

chocolate passion cake

serves 6

prep: 25 mins, plus 1 hr cooling

cook: 45 mins

What could be nicer than passion cake with added chocolate?
Rich and moist, this cake is fabulous with afternoon tea.

INGREDIENTS

butter, for greasing

5 eggs

generous ¾ cup superfine sugar

1 cup all-purpose flour

generous ⅜ cup unsweetened cocoa

6 oz/175 g carrots, peeled, finely
grated, and squeezed until dry

generous ⅜ cup chopped walnuts

2 tbsp corn oil

1½ cups medium-fat soft cheese

1½ cups confectioners' sugar

6 oz/175 g milk or semisweet
chocolate, melted (see pages 9–10)

cook's tip

The undecorated cake can be frozen
for up to 2 months. Thaw at room
temperature for 3 hours or preferably
overnight in the refrigerator.

1 Preheat the oven to
375°F/190°C. Lightly
grease and line the bottom of
an 8-inch/20-cm deep round
cake pan.

2 Place the eggs and
sugar in a large
heatproof bowl set over a pan
of gently simmering water
and, using an electric whisk,
whisk until the mixture is very

thick and the whisk leaves a
trail that lasts a few seconds
when lifted.

3 Remove the bowl from
the heat. Sift the flour
and cocoa into the bowl and
carefully fold in. Fold in the
carrots, walnuts, and corn
oil until the cake batter is
just blended.

4 Pour into the prepared
pan and bake in
the preheated oven for
45 minutes. Let cool slightly,
then turn out onto a wire rack
to cool completely.

5 Beat the soft cheese
and confectioners'
sugar together until blended,
then beat in the melted
chocolate. Split the cake in

half and sandwich together
again with half the chocolate
mixture. Cover the top of the
cake with the remainder of the
chocolate mixture, swirling it
with a knife. Let chill in the
refrigerator until required or
serve immediately.

caribbean chocolate cake

cook: 45–50 mins   **prep: 10 mins, plus 1 hr 20 mins cooling/setting**   **serves 12**

Chocolate and spice are combined in this light cake with a tasty preserved ginger topping, which is perfect for any time of the day.

cook's tip

If possible, this cake benefits from being kept in an airtight container for a day before eating to allow the flavors time to develop.

INGREDIENTS

4 oz/115 g butter, diced

scant 1½ cups self-rising flour

¼ cup unsweetened cocoa

1 tbsp ground ginger

1 tsp ground cinnamon

½ tsp baking soda

½ cup light brown sugar

2 eggs

1½ tbsp corn syrup

1½ tbsp milk

TOPPING

6 pieces preserved ginger, plus syrup

1 cup confectioners' sugar

1 tbsp rum

1 Preheat the oven to 325°F/160°C. Grease and line the bottom of a shallow 7-inch/18-cm square cake pan. Sift the flour, unsweetened cocoa, ground ginger, cinnamon, and baking soda into a large bowl. Add the butter and rub it in with your fingertips, then stir in the sugar. Make a well in the center.

2 Place the eggs in a separate bowl with the syrup and milk. Whisk together, then pour into the well in the dry ingredients and beat until smooth and glossy. Spoon the cake batter into the pan. Bake for 45–50 minutes, or until well risen and firm to the touch. Let stand in the pan for 30 minutes, then let cool completely on a wire rack.

3 For the topping, cut each piece of preserved ginger into quarters and arrange on top of the cake. Sift the confectioners' sugar into a bowl and stir in the rum and enough of the ginger syrup to make a smooth frosting. Drizzle the frosting over the cake and let set. Cut the cake into 12 squares to serve.

sachertorte

serves 8–10

prep: 25 mins, plus 2 hrs setting

cook: 1 hr 10 mins– 1 hr 25 mins

Sachertorte is a most famous Viennese speciality with a distinctive glazed finish. It is the perfect cake for a very special occasion.

INGREDIENTS

4 oz/115 g unsalted butter, softened, plus extra for greasing

6 oz/175 g semisweet chocolate, broken into pieces

3 tbsp black coffee

¾ cup golden superfine sugar

5 eggs, separated

1 cup all-purpose flour, sifted

4 tbsp apricot jelly

dash of lemon juice

1 tbsp water

FROSTING

⅜ cup golden superfine sugar

4 tbsp water

3½ oz/100 g semisweet chocolate, broken into pieces

variation

If making this cake for a special occasion, serve with fresh fruit. If apricot jelly is unavailable, you can use raspberry jelly instead.

cook's tip

The traditional glaze on this cake can be quite tricky. An easier method is to melt 6 oz/175 g semisweet chocolate and 2 tablespoons of light cream together, then spread over the cake and let set.

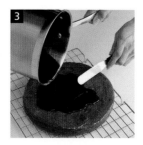

1 Preheat the oven to 325°F/160°C. Grease and line a 9-inch/23-cm round cake pan. Heat the chocolate in a pan with the coffee until melted, stir, and cool. Beat the butter and ⅜ cup of the sugar in a bowl until fluffy. Beat in the chocolate mixture and egg yolks. Stir in the flour. Whisk the egg whites in a separate bowl until stiff. Whisk in the

remaining sugar. Fold into the cake batter. Turn into the pan and bake for 1–1¼ hours, until firm. Let stand in the pan for 5 minutes. Turn out onto a wire rack to cool.

2 Slice the cake in half horizontally. Sandwich together with half the jelly. Heat the remaining jelly, lemon juice, and water in a pan until

the jelly has melted. Strain into a bowl then brush over the top and sides of the cake.

3 For the frosting, heat the sugar and water until boiling and stir until the sugar has dissolved. Remove from the heat, add the chocolate, and stir until smooth. Return to the heat and boil to a temperature of

241°F/116°C on a sugar thermometer. Remove from the heat, stir until the mixture stops bubbling, then pour all but 2 tablespoons quickly over the top of the cake, letting it flow down the sides. Smooth round the sides, but do not touch the top. When the frosting starts to set, warm the reserved frosting and drip "Sacher" over the top from the tip of a knife.

yule log

cook: 16–18 mins **prep: 35 mins, plus 30 mins cooling** **serves 8**

A chocolate yule log is a popular alternative to a Christmas cake and makes an eye-catching centerpiece for a festive table.

variation

Replace the Cointreau with brandy, or if you do not want to use any alcohol, use orange juice instead.

cook's tip

To roll the sponge, wring out a dish towel with hot water and place on a counter. Place waxed paper on top, sprinkled with superfine sugar. Put the sponge on top, peel off the lining paper, and roll up from a long side.

INGREDIENTS

butter, for greasing

3 eggs

generous ½ cup golden superfine sugar

generous ⅓ cup all-purpose flour

¼ cup unsweetened cocoa, plus extra to dust

Chocolate Caraque (see page 10)

2 oz/55 g white chocolate, melted (see pages 9–10)

confectioners' sugar, for dusting

SYRUP

generous ¼ cup golden superfine sugar

⅔ cup water

4 tbsp Cointreau

FROSTING

2 oz/55 g butter, softened

generous 1 cup confectioners' sugar, sifted

grated rind of 1 orange

1 tbsp Cointreau

BUTTERCREAM

1 tbsp unsweetened cocoa

1 tbsp boiling water

3 oz/85 g butter

1½ cups confectioners' sugar, sifted

1 Preheat the oven to 400°F/200°C. Grease and line an 8 x 12-inch/20 x 30-cm jelly roll pan. Whisk the eggs and sugar together until thick and a trail is left when the whisk is lifted. Sift the flour and unsweetened cocoa together into a separate bowl, then fold into the egg mixture. Turn into the pan and bake for 8–10 minutes, or until the cake springs back when lightly pressed. Roll up the sponge (see Cook's Tip) and let cool.

2 To make the syrup, heat the sugar and water in a pan until the sugar dissolves. Boil for 2 minutes. Stir in the Cointreau and let cool. Unroll the sponge and remove the paper. Sprinkle the sponge with syrup. To make the frosting, beat the butter until creamy. Beat in the other ingredients until smooth. Spread over the sponge and roll up.

3 To make the buttercream, place the cocoa in a heatproof bowl and stir in the water. Let cool. Beat the butter in a separate bowl until creamy. Gradually beat in the confectioners' sugar and cocoa until smooth. Cut off a quarter of the roll diagonally and attach to the side of the roll with buttercream. Cover the roll with buttercream and mark lines to represent bark. Cover with Chocolate Caraque. Pipe white chocolate spirals onto the ends. Dust with cocoa and confectioners' sugar.

german chocolate & hazelnut cake

serves 8 **prep: 10 mins, plus** ⟲ **30 mins cooling** **cook: 45–50 mins** ⏱

This is a classic German cake that tastes wonderful served as an afternoon snack with a hot cup of coffee or tea.

INGREDIENTS

6 oz/175 g unsalted butter, softened, plus extra for greasing

¾ cup dark brown sugar

scant 1 cup self-rising flour, plus extra for dusting

1 tbsp unsweetened cocoa

1 tsp allspice

3 eggs, beaten

1 cup ground hazelnuts

2 tbsp black coffee

confectioners' sugar, for dusting

cook's tip

A kugelhopf pan is a special fluted tube mold, available from specialist kitchenware stores. If you do not have one, you can use a 9-inch/23-cm ring mold instead.

1 Preheat the oven to 350°F/180°C. Grease and flour a 7½-inch/19-cm kugelhopf pan. Place the butter and brown sugar in a large mixing bowl and beat together until light and fluffy. Sift the self-rising flour, unsweetened cocoa, and allspice into a separate bowl.

2 Beat the eggs into the creamed batter, one at a time, adding 1 tablespoon of the flour mixture with the second and third eggs. Fold in the remaining flour mixture, ground hazelnuts, and coffee.

3 Turn into the prepared pan and bake in the oven for 45–50 minutes, or until the cake springs back when lightly pressed. Let stand in the pan for 10 minutes, then turn out onto a wire rack to cool completely. Dust generously with confectioners' sugar before serving.

orange & chocolate ring cake

cook: 40 mins

prep: 25 mins, plus 1 hr cooling/setting

serves 8–10

The addition of fresh oranges makes this cake very fruity and moist. It will be an instant favorite with friends and family.

cook's tip

You need not be skillful to frost a cake in this way—the more "spontaneous" it looks, the better! Just drizzle the frosting over the cake, then drizzle the chocolate over the top.

INGREDIENTS

6 oz/175 g butter, softened,
plus extra for greasing
2 small oranges
3 oz/85 g semisweet chocolate
scant 1½ cups self-rising flour
1½ tsp baking powder
¾ cup golden superfine sugar
3 eggs, beaten

GLAZE
2 cups confectioners' sugar
2 tbsp orange juice
2 oz/55 g semisweet chocolate,
broken into pieces

1 Preheat the oven to 325°F/160°C. Thoroughly grease a 3½-cup/850-ml fluted or plain ring mold. Grate the rind of 1 orange and set aside. Remove the rind of the other orange in fine strips with a zester and set aside. Cut the skin and pith from the oranges, then cut them into segments by cutting down between the membranes with a sharp knife. Chop the segments into small pieces, reserving as much juice as possible. Grate the chocolate onto a plate.

2 Sift the flour and baking powder into a large bowl. Add the butter, sugar, eggs, grated orange rind, and any reserved juice. Beat until smooth. Gently fold in the chopped oranges and grated chocolate. Spoon the batter into the pan. Bake in the oven for 40 minutes, or until well risen and golden brown. Let stand in the pan for 5 minutes, then turn out onto a wire rack and let cool.

3 To make the glaze, sift the confectioners' sugar into a bowl and stir in enough orange juice to make a coating consistency. Using a spoon, drizzle the frosting over the cake. Melt the chocolate (see pages 9–10) and drizzle over the cake. Sprinkle the reserved strips of orange rind on top. Let set before serving.

chocolate & vanilla marble cake

serves 10   **prep: 25 mins, plus** ↻ **1 hr cooling/setting**   **cook: 1 hr–1 hr 10 mins** ⏱

This cake looks impressive but it is easy to make. Just drag a toothpick through two contrasting cake batters to create a professional-looking marbled effect.

INGREDIENTS

8 oz/225 g butter, softened, plus extra for greasing

2 oz/55 g semisweet chocolate, broken into pieces

1 tbsp strong black coffee

generous 1½ cups self-rising flour

1 tsp baking powder

generous 1 cup golden superfine sugar

4 eggs, beaten

½ cup ground almonds

2 tbsp milk

1 tsp vanilla extract

FROSTING

4½ oz/125 g semisweet chocolate, broken into pieces

2 tbsp butter

2 tbsp water

variation

If you don't have a ring mold, use a 9-inch/23-cm deep round cake pan instead. Replace the frosting with a Fudge Sauce (see page 161).

cook's tip

If you would prefer a plainer cake, omit the chocolate frosting and simply dust the top of the cake with sifted confectioners' sugar before serving.

1 Preheat the oven to 350°F/180°C. Grease a 7-cup/1.7-liter ring mold. Place the chocolate and coffee in a heatproof bowl and set over a pan of gently simmering water until the chocolate has melted. Stir until smooth and let cool. Sift the flour and baking powder into a separate bowl. Add the butter, sugar, eggs, ground almonds, and milk. Beat together thoroughly until smooth.

2 Transfer one half of the cake batter to another bowl and stir in the vanilla extract. Stir the melted chocolate into the other half of the cake batter. Place spoonfuls of the 2 cake batters alternately into the prepared mold, then drag a toothpick through to create a marbled effect. Level the top. Bake in the oven for 50–60 minutes, or until well risen and the tip of a knife inserted into the center comes out clean. Let stand in the pan for 5 minutes, then turn out onto a wire rack to cool completely.

3 To make the frosting, place the chocolate, butter, and water in a heatproof bowl and set over a pan of simmering water until melted. Stir until smooth, then pour over the cake, working quickly to coat the top and sides. Let set before serving.

sunken drunken chocolate cake

cook: 40–45 mins

**prep: 15 mins, plus
30 mins cooling**

serves 8–10

*This dense rich cake contains no flour and will sink and crack
slightly when you take it out of the oven.*

variation

Serve as a dessert with vanilla ice
cream or fresh fruit, such as
strawberries and sliced peaches.

cook's tip

This cake is very fragile and
benefits from being chilled for at
least 10 minutes in the refrigerator
before serving. Any uneaten cake
should be covered with foil and
stored in the refrigerator.

INGREDIENTS

4 oz/115 g butter, diced,
plus extra for greasing

flour, for dusting

5 oz/140 g semisweet chocolate,
broken into pieces

2 tbsp brandy

⅜ cup golden superfine sugar

6 eggs, separated

1¼ cups ground almonds

1¼ cups whipped cream,
to decorate

ground cinnamon, for dusting

1 Preheat the oven
to 325°F/160°C. Grease
a 9-inch/23-cm springform
cake pan and line the bottom
with nonstick parchment
paper. Dust the sides with
flour. Place the chocolate and
brandy in a heatproof bowl
and set over a pan of
simmering water until the
chocolate has melted. Stir until
smooth, then let cool slightly.

2 Place the butter in a
separate bowl, add the
sugar and beat until light and
creamy. Add the egg yolks, one
at a time, beating well after
each addition, then stir in the
melted chocolate. Add the
ground almonds and beat in.
Place the egg whites in a large,
spotlessly clean, greasefree
bowl and whisk until stiff but
not dry. Stir 2 tablespoons of

the whisked egg whites into
the chocolate batter, then
carefully fold in the remainder.

3 Spoon the batter
into the prepared pan
and bake in the oven for
35–40 minutes, or until well
risen and just firm to the
touch. Let stand in the pan to
cool completely. When cold,
remove the cake from the pan

and peel away the lining paper,
then transfer to a serving plate.
Spoon whipped cream over the
top to decorate and dust with
a little cinnamon. Serve, cut
into slices.

mocha walnut meringue gâteau

serves 8 **prep: 25 mins, plus** ⏲ **1 hr cooling** **cook: 1 hr 35 mins** ⏲

This deliciously crisp nutty meringue contrasts wonderfully with its creamy, brandy-laced filling, and is perfect for any occasion.

INGREDIENTS

4 egg whites

generous 1 cup golden superfine sugar

½ cup shelled walnuts, finely chopped

FILLING

6 oz/175 g semisweet chocolate

1½ oz/40 g unsalted butter

2 tbsp strong black coffee

2 tbsp brandy

¾ cup whipping cream

confectioners' sugar, for dusting

variation

Instead of walnuts, add chopped toasted hazelnuts or ground almonds to the meringue.

cook's tip

Lining the baking sheets with non stick parchment paper makes it easier to remove the cooled meringues. Use a round-bladed knife to spread the meringues out on the baking sheets.

1 Preheat the oven to 275°F/140°C. Line 2 baking sheets with nonstick parchment paper. To make the meringue, place the egg whites in a large, clean, greasefree bowl and whisk until stiff but not dry. Whisk in half the sugar. Add the walnuts to the remaining sugar and mix together. Fold into the meringue mixture.

2 Spread the meringue into 2 x 8-inch/20-cm circles on the baking sheets. Bake in the preheated oven for 1½ hours, or until completely dry. Let cool in the oven.

3 To make the filling, break the chocolate into pieces and place in a heatproof bowl with the butter, coffee, and brandy. Set over a pan of gently simmering water until melted. Stir and let cool. Place the cream in a separate bowl and whip lightly, then stir in the chocolate mixture. Sandwich the meringue circles together with the chocolate cream. Dust lightly with sifted confectioners' sugar before serving.

chocolate almond cake

serves 8

prep: 1 hr, plus 2 hrs 30 mins cooling/setting

cook: 40 mins

Chocolate and almonds complement each other perfectly in this delicious cake. Be warned though, one slice will never be enough!

INGREDIENTS

6 oz/175 g butter, plus extra for greasing

6 oz/175 g semisweet chocolate, plus extra to decorate

generous ⅜ cup superfine sugar

4 eggs, separated

¼ tsp cream of tartar

6 tbsp self-rising flour

generous 1 cup ground almonds

1 tsp almond extract

4½ oz/125 g milk chocolate

2 tbsp butter

4 tbsp heavy cream

¼ cup toasted slivered almonds

---

cook's tip

To toast almonds, place the almonds on a foil-lined broiler rack and place under the preheated broiler for 3–5 minutes, turning frequently. Take care as they burn very easily.

1 Preheat the oven to 375°F/190°C. Grease and line the bottom of a 9-inch/23-cm round springform cake pan. Break the chocolate into pieces and place in a pan with the butter. Heat, stirring, until blended. Whisk ½ cup of the sugar and egg yolks together until pale and creamy. Add the chocolate, beating until mixed.

2 Sift the cream of tartar and flour together and fold into the chocolate cake batter with the ground almonds and almond extract.

3 Whisk the egg whites in a clean bowl until soft peaks form. Add the remaining superfine sugar and whisk for 2 minutes, or until thick and glossy. Fold the egg whites into the chocolate cake batter and spoon into the pan. Bake in the hot oven for 40 minutes, or until just springy to the touch. Let cool.

4 Heat the milk chocolate, butter, and cream together in a heatproof bowl set over a pan of gently simmering water. Remove from the heat and beat for 2 minutes. Let cool for 30 minutes. Transfer the cake to a serving plate, spread the top with the chocolate mixture, and sprinkle with the almonds. Melt a little semisweet chocolate (see pages 9–10) and use to drizzle over the cake. Let set for 2 hours before serving.

chocolate lamington cake

cook: 45 mins   **prep: 25 mins, plus 1 hr 20 mins cooling/setting**   **serves 8**

This recipe is based on a famous Australian cake named after Lord Lamington, a former Governor of Queensland.

cook's tip

When piping cream, use a large star-shaped tip. Hold the pastry bag in your hand and turn the top to come halfway down the sides of the bag. Fill and pull the sides of the bag up to the top.

INGREDIENTS

6 oz/175 g butter, plus extra
for greasing

scant 1 cup superfine sugar

3 eggs, lightly beaten

1 cup self-rising flour

2 tbsp unsweetened cocoa

1¾ oz/50 g semisweet chocolate,
broken into pieces

5 tbsp milk

1 tsp butter

generous 1 cup confectioners' sugar

8 tbsp dry unsweetened coconut

⅔ cup heavy cream, whipped

1 Preheat the oven to 350°F/180°C. Lightly grease a 1-lb/450-g loaf pan—preferably a long, thin pan measuring 3 x 10 inches/ 7.5 x 25 cm.

2 Beat the butter and sugar together in a bowl until light and fluffy. Gradually add the eggs, beating well after each addition. Sift the flour and cocoa together, then fold into the cake batter.

3 Pour the cake batter into the pan and level the top. Bake in the hot oven for 40 minutes, or until springy to the touch. Cool in the pan for 5 minutes, then turn out onto a wire rack to cool completely.

4 Place the chocolate, milk, and butter in a heatproof bowl and set over a pan of hot water. Stir until the chocolate has melted. Add the confectioners' sugar and beat until smooth. Let cool until the frosting is thick enough to spread, then spread it all over the cake. Sprinkle with the coconut and let set.

5 Cut a V-shaped wedge from the top of the cake. Place the cream in a pastry bag fitted with a plain or star tip and pipe the cream down the center of the gap left by the wedge. Replace the wedge of cake on top of the cream. Pipe another line of cream down either side of the wedge of cake, then serve.

almond & hazelnut gâteau

cook: 25 mins **prep: 1 hr, plus 1 hr 40 mins cooling/chilling** **serves 8**

This is a light, nutty gâteau sandwiched together with chocolate cream. Simple to create, it is a cake you are sure to make again and again as it will be a winner with both family and friends.

---

variation

If you are making this gâteau for a special occasion, add 1 tablespoon of rum or brandy to the filling.

---

cook's tip

When dusting with confectioners' sugar, use a small strainer or flour sifter to sift the sugar evenly over the top of the cake. This also prevents any lumps falling onto the cake.

INGREDIENTS

butter, for greasing

4 eggs

½ cup superfine sugar

½ cup ground almonds

½ cup ground hazelnuts

5½ tbsp all-purpose flour

scant ½ cup slivered almonds

confectioners' sugar, for dusting

FILLING

3½ oz/100 g semisweet chocolate

1 tbsp butter

1¼ cups heavy cream

1 Preheat the oven to 375°F/190°C. Grease and line the bottoms of 2 x 7-inch/18-cm round sandwich cake pans.

2 Whisk the eggs and superfine sugar together for 10 minutes, or until light and foamy and the whisk leaves a trail that lasts a few seconds when lifted.

3 Fold in the ground almonds and hazelnuts, sift the flour and fold in with a metal spoon or spatula. Pour into the prepared pans.

4 Sprinkle the slivered almonds over the top of one of the cakes, then bake both cakes in the preheated oven for 15–20 minutes, or until springy to the touch.

5 Let cool in the pans for 5 minutes, then turn out onto wire racks to cool completely.

6 To make the filling, melt the chocolate (see pages 9–10), remove from the heat, and stir in the butter. Let cool. Whip the cream until holding its shape, then fold in the chocolate until mixed.

7 Place the cake without the extra almonds on a serving plate and spread the filling over it. Let set slightly, then place the almond-topped cake on top of the filling and let chill in the refrigerator for 1 hour. Dust with confectioners' sugar and serve.

banana & chocolate teabread

serves 8

prep: 10 mins, plus 40 mins cooling

cook: 50–60 mins

This is a good cake to make when you have some overripe bananas in the fruit bowl. It is delicious served in slices with butter.

INGREDIENTS

4 oz/115 g butter, softened, plus extra for greasing

2 ripe bananas

⅜ cup golden superfine sugar

2 eggs

scant 1½ cups self-rising flour

¼ cup unsweetened cocoa

1 tsp baking powder

1–2 tbsp milk

generous ½ cup semisweet chocolate chips

butter, to serve (optional)

variation

Add ⅞ cup chopped walnuts or the same amount of chopped dates to the mixture at the end of Step 2.

cook's tip

To make it slightly easier and quicker, you can mix the ingredients in a food processor, then stir in the chocolate chips by hand, if you like.

1 Preheat the oven to 350°F/180°C. Grease and line a 2-lb/900-g loaf pan. Peel the bananas and place in a large bowl. Mash with a fork.

2 Add the butter, sugar, and eggs, then sift the flour, unsweetened cocoa, and baking powder into the bowl.

Beat vigorously until smooth, adding enough milk to give a reluctant dropping consistency. Stir in the chocolate chips.

3 Spoon the mixture into the prepared pan and bake in the oven for 50–60 minutes, or until well risen and the tip of a knife inserted in the center comes

out clean. Let stand in the pan for 5 minutes, then turn out onto a wire rack to cool completely. Serve sliced, with or without butter.

sicilian cassata

⏱ cook: 30–40 mins   ⏲ prep: 25 mins, plus   serves 8
                              9 hrs cooling/chilling

This rich cake, with a filling of ricotta cheese, candied fruit,
chopped nuts, and semisweet chocolate, is a speciality of Sicily.

variation

If Marsala wine is unavailable, use
dry sherry instead. Brandy would
also work well in this cake.

cook's tip

If possible, buy pieces of candied peel
and chop them yourself, rather than
using ready-chopped peel. Store the
cake in the refrigerator.

INGREDIENTS

6 oz/175 g butter, softened,
plus extra for greasing
generous 1 cup self-rising flour
2 tbsp unsweetened cocoa
1 tsp baking powder
scant 1 cup golden superfine sugar
3 eggs
confectioners' sugar, for dusting
Chocolate Curls (see page 10),
to decorate

FILLING

1 lb/450 g ricotta cheese
3½ oz/100 g semisweet
chocolate, grated
generous ½ cup golden superfine sugar
3 tbsp Marsala wine
⅓ cup chopped candied peel
2 tbsp almonds, chopped

1 Preheat the oven
to 375°F/190°C/. Grease
and line the bottom of a
7-inch/18-cm round cake pan.
Sift the flour, unsweetened
cocoa, and baking powder
into a large bowl. Add the
butter, sugar, and eggs and
beat together thoroughly until
smooth and creamy. Pour the
cake batter into the prepared
pan and bake in the oven for

30–40 minutes, or until well
risen and firm to the touch. Let
stand in the pan for 5 minutes,
then turn out onto a wire rack
to cool completely.

2 Wash and dry the cake
pan and grease and line
it again. To make the filling,
rub the ricotta through a
strainer into a bowl. Add the
grated chocolate, sugar, and

Marsala wine and beat
together until the mixture is
light and fluffy. Stir in the
candied peel and almonds.

3 Cut the thin crust off
the top of the cake
and discard. Cut the cake
horizontally into 3 layers. Place
the first slice in the prepared
pan and cover with half the
ricotta mixture. Repeat the

layers, finishing with a cake
layer. Press down lightly, cover
with a plate and a weight, and
let chill in the refrigerator for
8 hours, or overnight. To serve,
turn the cake out onto a
serving plate. Dust with
confectioners' sugar and
decorate with Chocolate Curls.

chocolate pear tart

serves 8 **prep: 25 mins, plus** ⏱ **1 hr cooling/chilling** **cook: 30 mins** ⏱

The classic partnership of chocolate and pears appears in many forms, both hot and cold. This tart will soon become a favorite.

INGREDIENTS

generous ⅝ cup all-purpose flour, plus extra for dusting

pinch of salt

2 tbsp superfine sugar

4 oz/115 g unsalted butter, diced

1 egg yolk

1 tbsp lemon juice

4 oz/115 g semisweet chocolate, grated

4 pears

½ cup light cream

1 egg, plus 1 egg yolk

½ tsp almond extract

3 tbsp superfine sugar

1 fresh mint sprig, to decorate

cook's tip

Before baking, place the tart on a large baking sheet as the filling may leak out slightly during cooking. The tart is also easier to remove from the oven if placed on a baking sheet.

1 Sift the flour and the salt into a large bowl. Add the superfine sugar and butter and mix well with a pastry blender or 2 forks until thoroughly incorporated. Stir in the egg yolk and lemon juice to form a dough. Form the dough into a ball, wrap in plastic wrap, and let chill in the refrigerator for 30 minutes.

2 Preheat the oven to 400°F/200°C. Roll out the dough on a lightly floured counter and use to line a 10-inch/25-cm loose-bottom tart pan. Sprinkle the grated chocolate over the base of the pastry shell. Peel the pears, cut them in half lengthwise, and remove the cores. Thinly slice each pear half crosswise and

fan the slices out slightly. Using a spatula, scoop up each sliced pear half and arrange in the pastry shell.

3 Beat the cream, egg, extra yolk, and almond extract together and spoon over the pears. Sprinkle the sugar over the tart.

4 Bake in the preheated oven for 10 minutes. Reduce the oven temperature to 350°F/180°C and bake for an additional 20 minutes, or until the pears are starting to caramelize and the filling is just set. Remove from the oven and let cool to room temperature before serving. Decorate with a fresh mint sprig and serve.

date & chocolate cake

cook: 40 mins   **prep: 25 mins, plus 20 mins cooling**   **serves: 6**

Moist and moreish, this fruity chocolate cake will prove to be a popular after-school snack.

variation

Replace the orange juice in the filling with the same quantity of lemon juice for a zestier flavor.

INGREDIENTS

4 oz/115 q unsalted butter

½ cup self-rising flour

4 oz/115 g semisweet chocolate

1 tbsp grenadine

1 tbsp corn syrup

generous ¼ cup superfine sugar

2 large eggs

2 tbsp ground rice

1 tbsp confectioners' sugar, to decorate

FILLING

⅔ cup dried dates, chopped

1 tbsp orange juice

1 tbsp raw sugar

⅛ cup blanched almonds, chopped

2 tbsp apricot jelly

1 Preheat the oven to 350°F/180°C. Grease and dust 2 x 7-inch/18-cm sandwich cake pans with a little extra butter and flour. Break the chocolate into pieces, then place the chocolate, grenadine, and syrup in the top of a double boiler or in a heatproof bowl set over a pan of barely simmering water. Stir over low heat until the chocolate has melted and the mixture is smooth. Remove the pan from the heat and let cool.

2 Beat the butter and superfine sugar together in a bowl until pale and fluffy. Gradually beat in the eggs, then beat in the chocolate mixture.

3 Sift the flour into another bowl and stir in the ground rice. Fold the 2 mixtures together.

4 Divide the cake batter between the pans and level the surface. Bake in a hot oven for 20–25 minutes, or until golden and firm to the touch. Turn out onto a wire rack to cool.

5 To make the filling, put all the ingredients into a pan and stir over low heat for 4–5 minutes, or until fully blended. Remove from the heat, let cool, then use the filling to sandwich the cakes together. Dust the top of the cake with confectioners' sugar and serve.

lemon & chocolate tart

serves 8–10   prep: 20 mins, plus 🕒 30 mins chilling   cook: 1 hr 15 mins 🕒

In this tart, a crisp chocolate pastry shell is the perfect foil for the smooth creamy lemon filling. It is the perfect end to a supper party.

INGREDIENTS

¾ cup all-purpose flour

¼ cup unsweetened cocoa

2¾ oz/75 g butter

¼ cup ground almonds

¼ cup golden superfine sugar

1 egg, beaten

Chocolate Curls (see page 10), to decorate

FILLING

4 eggs

1 egg yolk

1 cup golden superfine sugar

⅔ cup heavy cream

grated rind and juice of 2 lemons

---

variation

For an orange-flavored tart, substitute the grated rind and juice of 2 lemons with the grated rind and juice of 2 oranges.

---

cook's tip

Most lemons are waxed and sprayed before ending up in the supermarket, so if you are using grated lemon rind or zest in a cake or tart, try to buy unwaxed lemons.

1 Sift the flour and unsweetened cocoa into a food processor. Add the butter, almonds, sugar, and egg and process until the mixture forms a ball. Gather the dough together and press into a flattened ball. Place in the center of an 8½-inch/22-cm loose-bottom tart pan and press evenly over the bottom of the pan with your fingers, then work the pie dough up the sides with your thumbs. Allow any excess dough to go over the edge. Cover and let chill for 30 minutes.

2 Preheat the oven to 400°F/200°C. Trim off excess dough. Prick the dough base lightly with a fork, then line with parchment paper and fill with pie weights. Bake for 12–15 minutes, or until the dough no longer looks raw. Remove the weights and paper, return to the oven and bake for 10 minutes, or until the pastry is firm. Let cool. Reduce the oven temperature to 300°F/150°C.

3 To make the filling, whisk the whole eggs, egg yolk, and sugar together until smooth. Add the cream and whisk again, then stir in the lemon rind and juice. Pour the filling into the pastry shell and bake for 50 minutes, or until just set. When the tart is cooked, remove the tart ring and let cool. Decorate with Chocolate Curls before serving.

chocolate fudge tart

cook: 1 hr 15 mins   **prep: 15 mins, plus 30 mins cooling**   serves 6–8

This rich, fudgy tart is sure to become a favorite, and is quick and easy to prepare using ready-made pastry. Serve with cream.

---

variation

For a special treat, replace the ready-made pastry with Rich Chocolate Pie Dough (see page 13).

---

cook's tip

The best way to transfer the rolled out pie dough to the tart pan is to roll the dough gently onto the lightly floured rolling pin, lift it off the counter, and ease it into the pan.

INGREDIENTS

flour, for sprinkling
12 oz/350 g ready-made
unsweetened pie dough
confectioners' sugar, for dusting

1¾ cups golden granulated sugar
¾ cup all-purpose flour
½ tsp vanilla extract
6 eggs, beaten

FILLING
5 oz/140 g semisweet chocolate, finely chopped
6 oz/175 g butter, diced

TO DECORATE
⅔ cup whipped cream
ground cinnamon

1 Preheat the oven to 400°F/200°C. Roll out the pie dough on a lightly floured counter and use to line an 8-inch/20-cm deep loose-bottom tart pan. Prick the dough base lightly with a fork, then line with foil and fill with pie weights. Bake in the oven for 12–15 minutes, or until the dough no longer looks raw. Remove the beans and foil and bake for an additional 10 minutes, or until the dough is firm. Let cool. Reduce the oven temperature to 350°F/180°C.

2 To make the filling, place the chocolate and butter in a heatproof bowl and set over a pan of gently simmering water until melted. Stir until smooth, then remove from the heat and let cool. Place the sugar, flour, vanilla extract, and eggs in a separate bowl and whisk until well blended. Stir in the butter and chocolate mixture.

3 Pour the filling into the pastry shell and bake in the oven for 50 minutes, or until the filling is just set. Transfer to a wire rack to cool completely. Dust with confectioners' sugar before serving with whipped cream sprinkled lightly with cinnamon.

pine nut tartlets

serves 8   **prep: 40 mins, plus 1 hr 40 mins cooling/chilling**   **cook: 45 mins**

Pine nuts and orange rind are very popular ingredients in Mediterranean dishes—here they add a twist of flavor to these tarts

INGREDIENTS

1 quantity of Extra-rich Unsweetened
Pie Dough (see page 13)

all-purpose flour, for dusting

2 oz/55 g semisweet chocolate

5 tbsp unsalted butter

scant 1 cup plus 2 tbsp superfine sugar

6 tbsp light brown sugar

6 tbsp milk

3½ tbsp corn syrup

finely grated rind of 2 large oranges
and 2 tbsp freshly squeezed juice

1 tsp vanilla extract

3 large eggs, lightly beaten

scant ½ cup pine nuts

cook's tip

Cover the tartlets with a piece of parchment paper for the last 5 minutes of the cooking time if the dough is browning too much or starting to burn.

1 Make the pie dough (see page 13). Shape the dough into a ball, wrap in plastic wrap, and let chill in the refrigerator for 1 hour.

2 Preheat the oven to 400°F/200°C. Roll the dough out on a lightly floured counter into 8 circles, each 6 inch/15 cm across. Use to line 8 loose-bottom 4-inch/ 10-cm tartlet pans. Line each with parchment paper to fit and fill with dried beans. Let chill in the refrigerator for 10 minutes.

3 Bake in the hot oven for 5 minutes. Remove the paper and beans and bake for 8 minutes. Let cool on a wire rack. Reduce the oven temperature to 350°F/180°C.

4 Meanwhile, break the chocolate into small pieces and place in a pan over low heat. Add the butter and stir until blended.

5 Stir in the remaining ingredients. Place the tartlet shells on a baking sheet and spoon the filling into the shells. Bake in the hot oven for 25–30 minutes, or until the tops puff up and crack and feel set. Transfer to a wire rack and let cool for 15 minutes before unmolding. Serve warm or at room temperature.

crispy chocolate pie

cook: 35–40 mins

prep: 25 mins, plus 30 mins cooling

serves 6

The whiskey-flavored chocolate filling makes this scrumptious pie very moreish. It is an excellent dessert for serving at a dinner party.

cook's tip

Replace the whiskey with the same amount of brandy and replace the grated chocolate with Chocolate Curls (see page 10).

INGREDIENTS

2 tsp butter, for greasing

2 egg whites

generous 1 cup ground almonds

scant ¼ cup ground rice

generous ½ cup superfine sugar

¼ tsp almond extract

8 oz/225 g semisweet chocolate

4 egg yolks

½ cup confectioners' sugar

4 tbsp whiskey

4 tbsp heavy cream

⅔ cup whipped cream

2 oz/55 g semisweet chocolate, grated

1 Preheat the oven to 325°F/160°C. Grease and line the bottom of an 8-inch/20-cm tart pan. Whisk the egg whites in a clean bowl until stiff peaks form. Fold in the ground almonds, ground rice, superfine sugar, and almond extract. Spread the mixture over the base and sides of the pan. Bake in the oven for 15 minutes.

2 Meanwhile, place the chocolate in the top of a double boiler or in a heatproof bowl set over a pan of barely simmering water and stir over low heat until the chocolate has melted. Remove from the heat and let cool slightly, then beat in the egg yolks, confectioners' sugar, whiskey, and the cream until thoroughly incorporated.

3 Remove the tart pan from the oven and pour in the chocolate mixture. Cover, return to the oven, and bake for 20–25 minutes, or until set. Remove from the oven and let cool completely.

4 Mix the whipped cream and 1 oz/25 g of the grated chocolate together in a bowl, then use to decorate the top of the pie. Top with the remaining grated chocolate, then serve immediately.

small cakes & pastries

Large cakes and gâteaux can look spectacular, but there is something about a pile of dainty "finger" cakes or delicate pastries that shouts out, "Eat me!" This selection of mouthwatering recipes includes light and fancy offerings for elegant tea parties, such as Chocolate Ginger Meringues (see page 180) or Raspberry & Chocolate Éclairs (see page 168), while for everyday occasions and family appeal you can't go wrong with Cupcakes (see page 184), with white or semisweet chocolate varieties to choose from, or Chocolate Chip Brownies, with or without the wicked Fudge Sauce (see page 161), which are easy to make and are sure to disappear almost the moment you have finished making them.

Why not start the day with a little indulgence in the form of Pains au Chocolat (see page 177), warm and inviting from the oven, Pecan & Chocolate Crêpes (see page 169), or Double Chocolate Chunk Muffins (see page 162)—perfect for a weekend brunch? Many of these individual cakes and pastries also make wonderful desserts, served warm or cold. So bring your evening meal and day to a close in style with White Chocolate Tarts (see page 167) or Pistachio & Chocolate Phyllo Fingers (see page 174), served with freshly brewed coffee.

mocha brownies with sour cream frosting

makes 9 large or 16 small brownies

prep: 20 mins, plus 30 mins cooling

cook: 30 mins

A hint of coffee and sour cream in the topping give these brownies a more sophisticated flavor.

INGREDIENTS

2 oz/55 g butter, plus extra for greasing

4 oz/115 g semisweet chocolate, broken into pieces

¾ cup dark brown sugar

2 eggs

2 tbsp strong coffee, cooled

generous ½ cup all-purpose flour

½ tsp baking powder

pinch of salt

¼ cup shelled walnuts, chopped

FROSTING

4 oz/115 g semisweet chocolate, broken into pieces

⅔ cup sour cream

variation

These brownies can be made without the frosting and served warm with vanilla ice cream or whipped cream.

cook's tip

Do not leave the brownies to set in the refrigerator but leave them in the cake pan in a cool place. Store any unfrosted brownies in an airtight container for up to 3 days.

1 Preheat the oven to 350°F/180°C. Grease an 8-inch/20-cm square cake pan with butter and line with parchment paper. Place the chocolate and butter in a small heatproof bowl and set over a pan of gently simmering water until melted. Stir until smooth. Remove from the heat and let cool.

2 Beat the sugar and eggs together until pale and thick. Fold in the chocolate mixture and coffee. Mix well. Sift the flour, baking powder, and salt into the cake batter and fold in. Fold in the walnuts. Pour the cake batter into the pan and bake in the oven for 20–25 minutes, or until set. Let cool in the pan.

3 To make the frosting, melt the chocolate (see pages 9–10). Stir in the sour cream and beat until evenly blended. Spoon the topping over the brownies and make a swirling pattern with a spatula. Let set in a cool place. Cut into squares, then remove from the pan and serve.

chocolate chip brownies with fudge sauce

⏲ **cook: 55–60 mins**   ⏱ **prep: 25 mins**   **makes 9 large or 16 small brownies**

Semisweet chocolate, unsweetened cocoa, and white chocolate chips make these brownies a chocolate-lover's dream, and when served with a chocolate fudge sauce, they are stunning!

variation

The brownies can be left to cool completely and served as cakes without the fudge sauce.

cook's tip

To make a more richly flavored chocolate fudge sauce, use the same amount of light or dark brown sugar instead of golden superfine sugar.

INGREDIENTS

4 oz/115 g butter, plus extra
for greasing

4 oz/115 g semisweet chocolate,
broken into pieces

1⅓ cups golden superfine sugar

pinch of salt

1 tsp vanilla extract

2 large eggs

1 cup all-purpose flour

2 tbsp unsweetened cocoa

½ cup white chocolate chips

FUDGE SAUCE

2 oz/55 g butter

generous 1 cup golden superfine sugar

⅔ cup milk

generous 1 cup heavy cream

⅔ cup corn syrup

7 oz/200 g semisweet chocolate,
broken into pieces

1 Preheat the oven to 350°F/180°C. Grease and line the bottom of a 7-inch/18-cm square cake pan. Place the butter and chocolate in a small heatproof bowl and set over a pan of gently simmering water until melted. Stir until smooth. Let cool slightly. Stir in the sugar, salt, and vanilla extract. Add the eggs, one at a time, stirring well each time, until blended.

2 Sift the flour and unsweetened cocoa into the cake batter and beat until smooth. Stir in the chocolate chips, then pour the batter into the pan. Bake in the oven for 35–40 minutes, or until the top is evenly colored and a toothpick inserted into the center comes out almost clean. Let cool slightly.

3 To make the sauce, place the butter, sugar, milk, cream, and syrup in a small pan and heat gently until the sugar has dissolved. Bring to a boil and stir for 10 minutes, or until the mixture is caramel colored. Remove from the heat and add the chocolate. Stir until smooth. Cut the brownies into squares and serve immediately with the sauce.

double chocolate chunk muffins

makes 12   **prep: 15 mins, plus 40 mins cooling/setting**   **cook: 20 mins**

Muffins are very easy to make, as all the ingredients are mixed quickly together and then poured into the paper cases.

INGREDIENTS

scant 1½ cups all-purpose flour

¼ cup unsweetened cocoa, plus extra for dusting

1 tbsp baking powder

1 tsp ground cinnamon

generous ½ cup golden superfine sugar

6½ oz/185 g white chocolate, broken into pieces

2 eggs

generous ⅓ cup corn oil

1 cup milk

variation

Instead of white chocolate, use semisweet or milk chocolate to spread on top of the muffins and dust with ground cinnamon.

cook's tip

When stirring the muffin batter together, do not overstir or the muffins will be tough. The muffin batter should be quite lumpy.

1 Preheat the oven to 400°F/200°C. Line a 12-hole muffin pan with double muffin paper cases. Sift the flour, unsweetened cocoa, baking powder, and cinnamon into a large bowl. Stir in the sugar and 4½ oz/125 g of the white chocolate.

2 Place the eggs and oil in a separate bowl and whisk until frothy, then gradually whisk in the milk. Stir into the dry ingredients until just blended. Spoon the batter into the paper cases, filling each three-quarters full. Bake in the preheated oven for 20 minutes, or until well risen and springy to the touch. Let cool for 2 minutes, then remove the muffins and let cool on a wire rack.

3 Melt the remaining white chocolate (see pages 9–10) and spread over the muffins. Let set, then dust the tops with a little unsweetened cocoa and serve.

fudge nut muffins

cook: 25–30 mins

prep: 10 mins, plus 30 mins cooling

makes 12

Chewy pieces of fudge give these muffins a lovely texture and contrast with the crunchiness of the nuts.

variation

To make these muffins really chocolatey, substitute the vanilla fudge with milk or semisweet chocolate fudge, if you like.

INGREDIENTS

scant 2 cups all-purpose flour

4 tsp baking powder

⅜ cup golden superfine sugar

6 tbsp crunchy peanut butter

1 egg, beaten

2¼ oz/60 g butter, melted

¾ cup milk

5½ oz/150 g vanilla fudge, cut into small pieces

3 tbsp coarsely chopped unsalted peanuts

1 Preheat the oven to 400°F/200°C. Line a 12-hole muffin pan with double muffin paper cases. Sift the flour and baking powder into a bowl. Stir in the sugar. Add the peanut butter and stir until the mixture resembles bread crumbs.

2 Place the egg, butter, and milk in a separate bowl and beat together until blended, then stir into the dry ingredients until just blended. Lightly stir in the fudge pieces. Spoon the cake batter into the muffin cases.

3 Sprinkle the chopped peanuts on top and bake in the preheated oven for 20–25 minutes, or until well risen and firm to the touch. Let cool for 2 minutes, then remove the muffins to a wire rack to cool completely before serving.

chocolate butterfly cakes

serves 12   **prep: 15 mins, plus 30 mins cooling**   **cook: 15 mins**

Filled with a tangy lemon buttercream, these appealing cakes will be a favorite with adults and children alike.

INGREDIENTS

4½ oz/125 g soft margarine

scant ⅔ cup superfine sugar

1 cup self-rising flour

2 large eggs

2 tbsp unsweetened cocoa

1 oz/25 g semisweet chocolate, melted

confectioners' sugar, for dusting

BUTTERCREAM

3½ oz/100 g unsalted butter, softened

⅞ cup confectioners' sugar, sifted

grated rind of ½ lemon

1 tbsp lemon juice

variation

For a chocolate buttercream, beat the butter and confectioners' sugar together, then beat in 1 oz/25 g melted semisweet chocolate.

1 Preheat the oven to 350°F/180°C. Place 12 paper cake cases in a muffin pan. Place all of the ingredients for the cakes, except for the melted chocolate, in a large bowl and, using an electric whisk, mix until the cake batter is just smooth. Mix in the chocolate.

2 Spoon equal amounts of the cake batter into each paper case, filling them three-quarters full. Bake in the preheated oven for 15 minutes, or until springy to the touch. Transfer the cakes to a wire rack and let cool completely.

3 Meanwhile, make the buttercream. Place the butter in a large bowl and beat until fluffy, then gradually beat in the confectioners' sugar. Beat in the lemon rind and gradually add the lemon juice, beating well.

4 When cold, cut the top off each cake, using a serrated knife. Cut each cake top in half.

5 Spread or pipe the buttercream over the cut surface of each cake and push the 2 cut pieces of cake top into the buttercream to form wings. Sprinkle the cakes with confectioners' sugar and serve.

white chocolate tarts

cook: 20 mins   prep: 40 mins, plus   makes 12
                       1 hr 35 mins chilling

*These dainty little tarts are wonderful for serving after dinner with
coffee instead of chocolates, or even as a delicious afternoon treat.*

variation

For a touch of decadence, use Basic
Chocolate Pie Dough (see page 13).
You could place the white chocolate
in the filling with semisweet.

cook's tip

When buying vanilla beans, choose
beans that are shiny, pliable, and
sticky. The seeds have a stronger flavor
than the bean. Store a bean in a jar of
superfine sugar to flavor the sugar.

INGREDIENTS

generous 1 cup all-purpose flour, plus
extra for dusting
2 tbsp golden superfine sugar
5½ oz/150 g chilled butter, diced
2 egg yolks
2 tbsp cold water
semisweet Chocolate Curls
(see page 10), to decorate
unsweetened cocoa, for dusting

FILLING

1 vanilla bean
1¾ cups heavy cream
12 oz/350 g white chocolate,
broken into pieces

1 Place the flour and sugar in a bowl. Add the butter and rub it in until the mixture resembles fine bread crumbs. Place the egg yolks and water in a separate bowl and mix together. Stir into the dry ingredients and mix to form a dough. Knead for 1 minute, or until smooth. Wrap in plastic wrap and let chill for 20 minutes.

2 Preheat the oven to 400°F/200°C. Roll out the dough on a floured counter and use to line 12 tartlet molds. Prick the bases, cover, and let chill for 15 minutes. Line the cases with foil and pie weights and bake for 10 minutes. Remove the weights and foil and cook for an additional 5 minutes. Let cool.

3 To make the filling, split the vanilla bean lengthwise and scrape out the black seeds with a knife. Place the seeds in a pan with the cream and heat until almost boiling. Place the chocolate in a heatproof bowl and pour over the hot cream. Keep stirring until smooth. Whisk the mixture with an electric whisk until thickened and the whisk leaves a trail when lifted. Let chill in the refrigerator for 30 minutes, then whisk until soft peaks form. Divide the filling between the pastry shells and let chill for 30 minutes. Decorate with Chocolate Curls and dust with unsweetened cocoa.

raspberry & chocolate éclairs

makes 20–24

prep: 20 mins, plus ↺ 25 mins cooling/setting

cook: 40 mins ⏱

These small éclairs are perfect for serving at a summer tea party. They look particularly appealing arranged on a pretty serving plate.

INGREDIENTS

2 oz/55 g butter

⅔ cup water

½ cup all-purpose flour, sifted

2 eggs, beaten

FILLING AND TOPPING

¾ cup heavy cream

1 tbsp confectioners' sugar

¾ cup fresh raspberries

3 oz/85 g semisweet chocolate, broken into pieces

variation

Instead of piping the choux mixture, you can simply spoon it onto the dampened baking sheets.

cook's tip

The raw piped choux mixture can be made a few days ahead and frozen, then baked directly from the freezer for 5 minutes longer than usual.

1 Preheat the oven to 425°F/220°C. To make the dough, place the butter and water in a heavy-bottom pan and bring to a boil over low heat. Add the flour, all at once, and beat thoroughly until the mixture leaves the side of the pan. Let cool slightly, then vigorously beat in the eggs, a little at a time.

2 Spoon the mixture into a pastry bag fitted with a ½-inch/1-cm tip and pipe 20–24 x 3-inch/7.5-cm lengths onto dampened baking sheets. Bake in the preheated oven for 10 minutes, then reduce the oven temperature to 375°F/190°C and bake for an additional 20 minutes, or until crisp and golden brown. Split the side of each éclair to let the steam escape, and transfer to a wire rack to cool completely.

3 To make the filling, place the cream and confectioners' sugar in a bowl and whip until thick. Spoon into the éclairs. Place a few raspberries in each éclair. To make the topping, melt the chocolate (see pages 9–10) and spread a little on top of each éclair. Let set, then transfer to a large serving plate and serve.

pecan & chocolate crêpes

cook: 20 mins   **prep: 10 mins**   makes 12–16

*American-style crêpes studded with nuts and chocolate
are popular at any time of the day.*

variation

Serve the warm crêpes in stacks with a
generous helping of maple syrup
poured over and a spoonful of vanilla
ice cream on the top.

INGREDIENTS

generous 1½ cups self-rising flour

1 tsp baking powder

pinch of salt

1 egg

1¼ cups milk

1 tbsp butter, melted

½ tsp vanilla extract

2 tbsp golden superfine sugar

⅓ cup semisweet chocolate chips

¼ cup shelled pecans, chopped

corn oil, for frying

butter, to serve (optional)

1 Sift the flour, baking powder, and salt into a large bowl and make a well in the center. Place the egg and milk in a small bowl and mix, pour into the well in the dry ingredients and whisk to make a thick, smooth batter.

2 Beat in the melted butter and vanilla extract, then stir in the superfine sugar, chocolate chips, and chopped pecans. Heat a teaspoon of corn oil in a large skillet or flat grill pan. Drop large tablespoonfuls of the batter into the hot pan to make crêpes 3-inches/ 7.5-cm across. Cook over medium heat for 3 minutes, or until small bubbles appear on the surface of each crêpe.

3 Turn with a spatula and cook for an additional 2–3 minutes, or until golden. Keep the crêpes warm by wrapping in foil or paper towels while cooking the remainder of the batter. Serve as they are, or with butter.

banana cream profiteroles

⏱ **cook: 30 mins**　　　　　⏲ **prep: 45 mins, plus 15 mins cooling**　　　　　**serves 4**

Profiteroles are a very popular choice. In this recipe they are filled with a delicious banana-flavored cream and served with a rich chocolate sauce—the perfect combination!

variation

Replace the banana-flavored cream with 1¼ cups whipped cream. Alternatively, fill with chocolate ice cream.

cook's tip

Don't make these profiteroles too far in advance. For an elegant presentation, arrange the filled profiteroles in a conical shape in a glass serving dish, pour the sauce over the top, and serve immediately.

INGREDIENTS

CHOUX PASTRY
5 tbsp butter, cut into small pieces, plus extra for greasing
⅔ cup water
½ cup strong all-purpose flour, sifted
2 eggs

SAUCE
3½ oz/100 g semisweet chocolate, broken into pieces
2 tbsp water
4 tbsp confectioners' sugar
2 tbsp unsalted butter

FILLING
1¼ cups heavy cream
1 banana
2 tbsp confectioners' sugar
2 tbsp banana-flavored liqueur

1 Preheat the oven to 425°F/220°C. Grease a baking sheet and sprinkle with a little water. To make the pastry, place the water in a pan. Add the butter and heat gently until the butter melts, then bring to a rolling boil. Remove from the heat and add the flour all at once, beating well until the mixture leaves the sides of the pan and forms a ball. Let cool slightly, then gradually beat in the eggs to form a smooth, glossy mixture. Spoon the mixture into a large pastry bag fitted with a ½-inch/1-cm plain tip.

2 Pipe 18 small balls of the mixture onto the baking sheet, allowing enough room for expansion during cooking. Bake in the preheated oven for 15–20 minutes, or until crisp and golden. Remove from the oven and make a small slit in each one for steam to escape. Let cool on a wire rack.

3 To make the sauce, place all the ingredients in a heatproof bowl and set over a pan of simmering water until smooth.

4 To make the filling, whip the cream until soft peaks form. Mash the banana with the sugar and liqueur, then fold into the cream. Place the mixture in a pastry bag fitted with a ½-inch/1-cm plain tip and pipe into the profiteroles. Serve immediately with the sauce poured over.

chocolate dairy wraps

makes 6 **prep: 15 mins, plus 30 mins cooling** ⟳ **cook: 6–8 mins** ⏲

*Light chocolate sponge is wrapped round a dairy cream filling.
These individual cakes can be served for dessert. If you like*

INGREDIENTS

2 eggs

4 tbsp superfine sugar

6 tbsp all-purpose flour

1½ tbsp unsweetened cocoa

4 tbsp apricot jelly

⅔ cup heavy cream, whipped

confectioners' sugar, for dusting

---

cook's tip

To ensure good results, remove the eggs from the refrigerator and allow them to return to room temperature before using.

1 Preheat the oven to 425°F/220°C. Line 2 baking sheets with parchment paper. Whisk the eggs and sugar together until the mixture is very light and fluffy and the whisk leaves a trail when lifted.

2 Sift the flour and cocoa together, then using a metal spoon or spatula, gently

fold it into the eggs and sugar mixture in a figure-of-eight movement.

3 Drop rounded tablespoons of the cake batter onto the prepared baking sheets and spread them into oval shapes, allowing enough room for expansion during cooking.

4 Bake in the preheated oven for 6–8 minutes, or until springy to the touch. Let cool on the baking sheets.

5 When cold, slide the cakes onto a damp dish towel and let stand until cold. Carefully remove them from the dampened paper. Spread the flat side of the cakes with

jelly, then spoon or pipe the whipped cream down the center of each one.

6 Fold the cakes in half and place them on a serving plate. Sprinkle them with confectioners' sugar and serve.

pistachio & chocolate phyllo fingers

makes 20   **prep: 10 mins, plus** ⟲ **10 mins cooling**   **cook: 20 mins** ⏱

The combination of pistachios and rose water give these crisp little pastries a delicate Middle Eastern flavor.

INGREDIENTS

2 oz/55 g butter, melted, plus extra for greasing

10 sheets of phyllo pastry dough, measuring 7 x 12 inches/18 x 30 cm

confectioners' sugar, for dusting

FILLING

¼ cup shelled pistachios, coarsely ground

½ cup ground hazelnuts

2 tbsp golden granulated sugar

1 tbsp rose water

2 oz/55 g semisweet chocolate, grated

variation

Replace the pistachios with almonds and the rose water with orange flower water. You can also add a few raisins to the filling.

cook's tip

Once phyllo pastry dough is removed from its packaging, it quickly dries out. To prevent this happening, cover the pastry sheets with a clean dish towel.

1 Preheat the oven to 350°F/180°C. Grease 2 baking sheets. Place the dry filling ingredients in a bowl with the sugar, rose water, and chocolate, and mix together. Cut each sheet of phyllo pastry dough in half lengthwise. Pile the rectangles on top of each other and cover with a dish towel.

2 Brush the top sheet of the phyllo pastry dough with a little of the melted butter. Spread a teaspoon of the filling along one short end of the rectangle. Fold the long sides in, slightly over the filling, and roll up from the filling end. Place the phyllo finger on a prepared baking sheet, seam-side down.

3 Repeat with the remaining dough and filling, then brush the tops with melted butter. Bake in the oven for 20 minutes, or until crisp and very lightly colored. Transfer to a wire rack to cool Dust with a little sifted confectioners' sugar and serve immediately.

pains au chocolat

cook: 15–20 mins   **prep: 40 mins, plus 7 hrs rising/chilling**   **makes 8**

There is nothing more irresistible than the sight and smell of freshly baked pains au chocolat emerging from the oven.

variation

Substitute the semisweet chocolate with the same quantity of milk chocolate, or use chocolate chips.

cook's tip

If you are making the pains au chocolat for breakfast, prepare them the night before, cover, and refrigerate overnight. Leave at room temperature for 30 minutes before baking.

INGREDIENTS

3½ oz/100 g butter, plus extra for greasing

scant 2 cups white bread flour, plus extra for dusting

1 tsp salt

2 tsp active dry yeast

¾ cup milk

2 tbsp golden superfine sugar

1 tbsp oil, plus extra for brushing

4 oz/115 g semisweet chocolate, coarsely chopped

GLAZE

1 egg yolk

2 tbsp milk

1 Grease a baking sheet. Sift the flour and salt into a bowl and stir in the yeast. Make a well in the center. Heat the milk in a pan until tepid. Add the sugar and oil and stir until the sugar has dissolved. Stir into the flour and mix well. Turn the dough out onto a lightly floured counter and knead until smooth, then place in an oiled bowl. Cover and let rise in a warm place for 2–3 hours, or until doubled in size.

2 Knead on a floured counter and roll into a rectangle 3 times as long as it is wide. Divide the butter into thirds. Dot one portion over the top two-thirds of the dough, leaving a ½-inch/1-cm margin round the edges. Fold the lower third up and the top third down. Seal the edges. Give the dough a half-turn. Roll into a rectangle. Repeat the process twice, then fold in half. Put into an oiled plastic bag. Let chill for 1 hour.

3 Preheat the oven to 425°F/220°C. Cut the dough in half and roll out into 2 rectangles of 12 x 6 inches/30 x 15 cm. Cut each half into 4 rectangles of 6 x 3 inches/15 x 7.5 cm. Sprinkle chocolate along one short end of each and roll up. Place on the baking sheet in a warm place for 2–3 hours, or until doubled in size. To glaze, mix the egg yolk and milk and brush over the rolls. Bake for 15–20 minutes, or until golden and well risen.

chocolate coconut squares

makes 9   prep: 15 mins, plus ⟳   cook: 35 mins ⟳
                 1 hr cooling/setting

*These cookies consist of a chewy coconut layer resting on a crisp
chocolate cracker base, cut into squares to serve.*

INGREDIENTS

6 tbsp butter or margarine, plus extra
for greasing

8 oz/225 g semisweet chocolate

graham crackers

6 oz/175 g canned evaporated milk

1 egg, beaten

1 tsp vanilla extract

2 tbsp superfine sugar

6 tbsp self-rising flour, sifted

1 cup dry unsweetened coconut

1¾ oz/50 g semisweet chocolate

(optional)

variation

Add 1 oz/25 g melted white chocolate
to the mixture in Step 3. Alternatively,
color the mixture pink with 1 teaspoon
of red food coloring.

cook's tip

Store the coconut squares in an
airtight container for up to 4 days.
They can be frozen, undecorated for
up to 2 months. Thaw at room
temperature before eating.

1 Preheat the oven to 375°F/190°C. Grease and line the bottom of a shallow 8-inch/20-cm square cake pan. Place the crackers in a plastic bag and crush with a rolling pin. Alternatively, place them in a food processor and process until crushed.

2 Melt the butter or margarine in a pan and stir in the crushed crackers until well blended. Press the mixture into the bottom of the cake pan.

3 Beat the evaporated milk, egg, vanilla extract, and sugar together until smooth. Stir in the flour and dry unsweetened coconut. Pour the mixture over the cracker base and level the top. Bake in the preheated oven for 30 minutes, or until the coconut topping is firm and just golden.

4 Let cool in the cake pan for 5 minutes, then cut into 9 squares. Let cool completely in the pan. Carefully remove the squares from the pan and place them on a board. Melt the semisweet chocolate (see pages 9–10) and drizzle it over the squares to decorate them. Let the chocolate set before serving.

chocolate ginger meringues

makes 8 **prep: 15 mins, plus 1 hr setting** **cook: 1 hr 35 mins**

These meringues are flecked with chocolate and sandwiched with a delicious ginger flavored cream.

INGREDIENTS

8 oz/225 g semisweet chocolate

4 egg whites

generous 1 cup golden superfine sugar

FILLING

1¼ cups heavy cream

3 pieces preserved ginger, finely chopped, plus 1 tbsp ginger syrup from the jar

cook's tip

Take care not to overwhisk the meringue mixture. Add the sugar a little at a time, whisking after each addition, then whisk in the grated chocolate with care.

1 Preheat the oven to 250°F/120°C. Line 2 baking sheets with nonstick parchment paper. Grate half the chocolate. Place the egg whites in a large, clean, greasefree bowl and whisk until stiff but not dry. Whisk in half the sugar, a little at a time. Mix the grated chocolate with the remaining sugar. Fold into the mixture.

2 Pipe or spoon 16 tablespoonfuls of the meringue mixture onto the prepared baking sheets. Bake in the preheated oven for 1½ hours, or until dry. Transfer to wire racks to cool. Melt the remaining chocolate (see pages 9–10) and spread a little over the base of each meringue. Leave the meringues on wire racks to set.

3 To make the filling, place the cream in a bowl and whip until thick. Stir in the chopped ginger and ginger syrup. Sandwich the meringues together in pairs with the ginger cream before serving.

banana & chocolate triangles

⏲ **cook: 14–16 mins**   ◔ **prep: 15 mins**   **makes 12**

These crisp little pockets can be served as a tasty party snack, or with coffee at the end of a meal.

variation

For an extra special chocolate sauce, add 1 tablespoon of brandy to the cream and chocolate in the pan in Step 3. Proceed as in main recipe.

INGREDIENTS

1 banana

2 tbsp semisweet chocolate chips

4 sheets of phyllo pastry dough, measuring 7 x 12 inches/18 x 30 cm

2 oz/55 g butter, melted

SAUCE

⅔ cup light cream

2 oz/55 g semisweet chocolate, broken into pieces

1 Preheat the oven to 350 F/180 C. Peel the banana, place in a bowl, and mash with a fork. Stir in the chocolate chips. Cover the phyllo pastry dough sheets with a dish towel to prevent them drying out. Brush a phyllo rectangle with melted butter and cut lengthwise into 3 strips, 2½ inches/6 cm wide.

2 Spoon a little of the banana mixture onto the bottom end of each strip, then fold the corner of the pastry over to enclose it in a triangle. Continue folding along the whole length of the strip to make a triangular pocket. Place on a large baking sheet with the seam underneath. Repeat with the remaining pastry

dough and filling. Bake in the oven for 10–12 minutes, or until golden brown.

3 To make the sauce, place the cream and chocolate in a pan and heat gently until the chocolate has melted. Stir until smooth. Serve the pastries immediately with the sauce.

chocolate hazelnut palmiers

⏱ **cook: 10–15 mins**   ⏲ **prep: 5 mins, plus 30 mins cooling**   **makes 26**

These delicious chocolate and hazelnut cookies are very simple to make, and they are ideal for birthday parties. For very young children, leave out the chopped nuts.

variation

For an extra chocolate flavor, dip the palmiers in melted semisweet chocolate to half-cover each cookie.

cook's tip

When rolling out dough on the counter, only use a small amount of flour as too much flour will affect the consistency of the dough.

INGREDIENTS

butter, for greasing

13 oz/375 g ready-made puff pastry dough

all-purpose flour, for dusting

8 tbsp chocolate hazelnut spread

scant ⅓ cup chopped toasted hazelnuts

2 tbsp superfine sugar

1 Preheat the oven to 425°F/220°C. Lightly grease a baking sheet. Roll out the puff pastry dough on a floured counter to a rectangle measuring 15 x 9 inches/ 38 x 23 cm.

2 Using a spatula, spread the chocolate spread over the puff pastry. Sprinkle the hazelnuts over the top.

3 Roll up one long side of the puff pastry to the center, then roll up the other side so that they meet in the center. Where the pieces meet, dampen the edges with water to join them. Using a sharp knife, cut into thin slices. Place each slice onto the prepared baking sheet and flatten slightly with a spatula. Sprinkle the slices with the sugar.

4 Bake in the preheated oven for 10–15 minutes, or until golden. Transfer to a wire rack to cool, then serve.

cupcakes

makes about 20   prep: 20 mins, plus 1 hr cooling/setting   cook: 35 mins

These tasty little cakes are light and moist with a tempting fudgy chocolate topping. Perfect for serving at any time of the day.

INGREDIENTS

generous ¾ cup water

3 oz/85 g butter

⅜ cup golden superfine sugar

1 tbsp corn syrup

3 tbsp milk

1 tsp vanilla extract

1 tsp baking soda

2 tbsp unsweetened cocoa

generous 1½ cups all-purpose flour

FROSTING

1¾ oz/50 g semisweet chocolate, broken into pieces

4 tbsp water

1¾ oz/50 g butter

1¾ oz/50 g white chocolate, broken into pieces

3 cups confectioners' sugar

TO DECORATE

candied rose petals

candied violets

variation

Instead of the candied flower petals, the cakes could be decorated with Chocolate Curls (see page 10) or chopped hazelnuts.

cook's tip

It is worthwhile investing in a set of cook's measuring spoons. Accuracy is particularly important when measuring baking soda.

1 Preheat the oven to 350°F/180°C. Place paper cake cases in 2 muffin pans. Place the water, butter, sugar, and syrup in a pan. Heat gently, stirring, until the sugar has dissolved, then bring to a boil. Reduce the heat and cook gently for 5 minutes. Remove from the heat and let cool. Place the milk and vanilla extract in a bowl. Add the baking soda and stir to dissolve. Sift the unsweetened cocoa and flour into a separate bowl and add the syrup mixture. Stir in the milk and beat until smooth.

2 Carefully spoon the batter into the paper cases to within two-thirds of the tops. Bake in the oven for 20 minutes, or until well risen and firm to the touch. Let cool on a wire rack. To make the frosting, place the semisweet chocolate in a small heatproof bowl with half the water and half the butter and set the bowl over a pan of gently simmering water until melted. Stir until smooth and let stand over the water. Repeat with the white chocolate and remaining water and butter.

3 Stir half the confectioners' sugar into each bowl and beat until smooth and fudgy. Divide the frostings between the cakes, filling to the top of the paper cases. Let cool, then place a rose petal on each of the semisweet chocolate frosted cakes and a violet on each white chocolate frosted cake. Let set before serving.

chocolate biscuits

makes 9   **prep: 10 mins** ⏱   **cook: 10–12 mins** ⏱

A plain biscuit mixture is transformed into a chocoholic's treat by the simple addition of chocolate chips. Split in half, spread with a spoonful of whipped cream, and serve with afternoon tea.

INGREDIENTS

5 tbsp butter, plus extra for greasing

1½ cups self-rising flour, sifted

1 tbsp superfine sugar

generous ¼ cup chocolate chips

about ⅔ cup milk

all-purpose flour, for dusting

cook's tip

To be at their best, all biscuits should be freshly baked and served warm. Split the warm biscuits and spread them with a little chocolate and hazelnut spread or a good spoonful of whipped cream.

1 Preheat the oven to 425°F/220°C. Lightly grease a baking sheet. Place the flour in a large bowl. Cut the butter into small pieces, add it to the flour, and rub it in with your fingertips until the mixture resembles fine bread crumbs. Stir in the superfine sugar and chocolate chips. Mix in enough milk to form a soft dough.

2 Roll out the dough on a lightly floured counter to form a rectangle measuring 4 x 6 inches/10 x 15 cm, 1 inch/2.5 cm thick, then cut into 9 squares.

3 Place the biscuits on the prepared baking sheet, allowing room for expansion during cooking. Brush with a little milk and bake in the preheated oven for 10–12 minutes, or until the biscuits are risen and golden. Let cool slightly and serve.

chocolate boxes

cook: 5 mins

prep: 20 mins, plus 40 mins chilling/setting

serves 4

Guests will think you have spent hours creating these lovely little chocolate boxes, but a few tricks, such as ready-made cake, make them quick to put together.

cook's tip

For the best results, keep the boxes well chilled in the refrigerator and fill and decorate them just before you want to serve them.

INGREDIENTS

8 oz/225 g semisweet chocolate

8 oz/225 g ready-made plain or chocolate cake

2 tbsp apricot jelly

⅔ cup heavy cream

1 tbsp maple syrup

3½ oz/100 g prepared fresh fruit, such as small strawberries, raspberries, kiwifruit, or red currants

1 Melt the semisweet chocolate (see pages 9–10) and spread it evenly over a large sheet of parchment paper. Let harden in a cool room.

2 When just set, cut the chocolate into 2-inch/5-cm squares with a sharp knife and carefully remove from the paper. Make sure that your hands are as cool as possible and handle the chocolate as little as possible.

3 Cut the cake into 2 x 2-inch/5-cm cubes, then cut each cube in half. Place the apricot jelly in a pan and heat gently until warm, then brush it over the sides of the cake cubes. Press a chocolate square onto each side of the cake cubes to make 4 chocolate boxes with cake at the bottom. Let chill for 20 minutes.

4 Whip the cream with the maple syrup until just holding its shape, then spoon a little of the mixture into each chocolate box.

5 Decorate the top of each box with the prepared fruit. If liked, the fruit can be partially dipped into melted chocolate and left to harden before being placed into the boxes.

cookies

Homemade cookies cost a fraction of ready-made ones and they taste so much better. They are easy to make, too. Just a few very simple ingredients will produce large quantities of delicious cookies, and no special equipment or baking pan are required for most of the recipes in this section. Children will enjoy helping to make them, and although it might be difficult to stop them eating them all, they could wrap some in pretty paper or pack them in an attractive container to give them as gifts. Homemade cookies will also be warmly received at fund-raising events such as fêtes and bazaars. The following recipes include specialities from round the world, such as spicy Lebkuchen (see page 204) from Germany, sticky Panforte di Siena (see page 226), and festive Chocolate & Nut Crescents (see page 208) from Greece. There are also all-time classics, such as shortbread and florentines, as well as variations on everyone's favorite, the chocolate chip cookie.

apricot & chocolate chip cookies

cook: 13–15 mins   prep: 20 mins, plus 30 mins cooling   makes 12–14

The apricots in these deliciously moist cookies give them a lovely fruity flavor. If there are any left, store in an airtight container.

variation

As an alternative to dried apricots, try other dried fruit such as dried cranberries, cherries, or raisins.

cook's tip

When baking, it is important to preheat the oven before the cookies and cakes are baked, otherwise they will not cook properly.

INGREDIENTS

3 oz/85 g butter, softened, plus extra for greasing

2 tbsp golden granulated sugar

¼ cup light brown sugar

½ tsp vanilla extract

1 egg, beaten

generous 1 cup self-rising flour

4 oz/115 g semisweet chocolate, coarsely chopped

⅔ cup no-soak dried apricots, coarsely chopped

1 Preheat the oven to 350°F/180°C. Grease 2 baking sheets. Place the butter, granulated sugar, brown sugar, and vanilla extract in a bowl and beat together. Gradually beat in the egg until light and fluffy.

2 Sift the flour over the cookie batter and fold in, then fold in the chocolate and apricots.

3 Put tablespoonfuls of the cookie batter onto the prepared baking sheets, allowing space for the cookies to spread. Bake in the oven for 13–15 minutes, or until crisp outside but still soft inside. Let cool on the baking sheets for 2 minutes, then transfer to wire racks to cool completely.

chocolate chip oaties

makes about 20

prep: 15 mins, plus 30 mins cooling

cook: 15 mins

Rolled oats give a light texture and a nutty flavor to these cookies. They are superb if served with a cup of fresh coffee.

INGREDIENTS

4 oz/115 g butter, softened, plus extra for greasing

½ cup firmly packed light brown sugar

1 egg

1 cup rolled oats

1 tbsp milk

1 tsp vanilla extract

scant 1 cup all-purpose flour

1 tbsp unsweetened cocoa

½ tsp baking powder

6 oz/175 g semisweet chocolate, broken into pieces

6 oz/175 g milk chocolate, broken into pieces

variation

Replace the semisweet and milk chocolate with 1 cup milk chocolate chips and 1 cup chopped pecans.

cook's tip

After baking, cookies must be left on the baking sheet for 2 minutes as this ensures that they do not fall apart when transferred to a wire rack to cool.

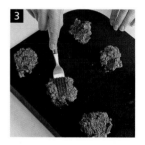

1 Preheat the oven to 350°F/180°C. Grease 2 baking sheets. Place the butter and sugar in a bowl and beat together until light and fluffy.

2 Beat in the egg, then add the oats, milk, and vanilla extract. Beat together until well blended. Sift the flour, unsweetened cocoa, and baking powder into the cookie batter and stir. Stir in the chocolate pieces.

3 Place dessertspoonfuls of the cookie batter on the prepared baking sheets and flatten slightly with a fork. Bake in the preheated oven for 15 minutes, or until slightly risen and firm. Let cool on the baking sheets for 2 minutes, then transfer to wire racks to cool completely.

double chocolate chip cookies

makes about 24   **prep: 15 mins, plus 20 mins cooling**   **cook: 10–12 mins**

Boasting both white and semisweet chocolate chips, these cookies are the ultimate treat for chocolate-lovers.

INGREDIENTS

7 oz/200 g butter, softened,
plus extra for greasing

1 cup golden superfine sugar

½ tsp vanilla extract

1 large egg

generous 1½ cups all-purpose flour

pinch of salt

1 tsp baking soda

⅔ cup white chocolate chips

⅔ cup semisweet chocolate chips

---

cook's tip

If you prefer a crisp cookie, rather than soft inside, cook them for a little bit longer, about 13–15 minutes, then proceed as in main recipe.

1 Preheat the oven to 350°F/180°C. Grease 2 baking sheets with butter. Place the butter, sugar, and vanilla extract in a large bowl and beat together. Gradually beat in the egg until the cookie batter is light and fluffy.

2 Sift the flour, salt, and baking soda over the cookie batter and fold in. Fold in the chocolate chips.

3 Drop dessertspoonfuls of the cookie batter onto the prepared baking sheets, allowing room for expansion during cooking. Bake in the oven for 10–12 minutes, or until crisp outside but still soft inside. Let cool on the baking sheets for 2 minutes, then transfer to wire racks to cool completely.

white chocolate cookies

cook: 10–12 mins

prep: 15 mins, plus 30 mins cooling

makes 24

These chunky cookies melt in the mouth and the white chocolate gives them a deliciously rich flavor.

variation

Replace the white chocolate with the same amount of semisweet or milk chocolate, if you prefer.

INGREDIENTS

4½ oz/125 g butter, softened, plus extra for greasing

⅝ cup firmly packed soft brown sugar

1 egg, beaten

generous 1¼ cups self-rising flour

pinch of salt

4½ oz/125 g white chocolate, coarsely chopped

generous ¼ cup Brazil nuts, chopped

1 Preheat the oven to 375°F/190°C. Lightly grease several baking sheets, enough to accommodate 24 cookies. Beat the butter and sugar together in a large bowl until light and fluffy. Gradually add the beaten egg to the cookie batter, beating well after each addition.

2 Sift the flour and salt into the cookie batter and blend well. Stir in the white chocolate chunks and the chopped Brazil nuts.

3 Drop heaped teaspoons of the batter onto the baking sheets. Do not put more than 6 teaspoons of the batter onto each sheet as they will spread during cooking.

4 Bake in the preheated oven, for 10–12 minutes, or until just golden brown. Transfer the cookies to wire racks and let stand until completely cold before serving.

chocolate pretzels

cook: 20 mins **prep: 30 mins, plus 1 hr 15 mins chilling/setting** **makes 30**

If you thought of pretzels as savories, then think again. These are fun to make and prove that pretzels come in a sweet variety, too.

---

variation

For a change, dip the whole pretzel in the melted chocolate and sprinkle the tops with chopped nuts.

---

cook's tip

The pretzels can be stored in an airtight container for up to 3 days. Make sure the pretzels are not too close together in the container, otherwise they may stick to each other.

INGREDIENTS

3½ oz/100 g unsalted butter, plus extra for greasing

½ cup superfine sugar

1 egg

1½ cups all-purpose flour

2 tbsp unsweetened cocoa

TO FINISH

1 tbsp butter

3½ oz/100 g semisweet chocolate

confectioners' sugar, for dusting

1 Lightly grease a baking sheet. Beat the butter and sugar together in a large bowl until light and fluffy. Beat in the egg. Sift the flour and unsweetened cocoa together and gradually beat in to form a soft dough. Use your fingers to incorporate the last of the flour and bring the dough together. Let chill in the refrigerator for 15 minutes.

2 Preheat the oven to 375°F/190°C. Break pieces from the dough and roll into sausage shapes 4-inches/10-cm long and ¼-inch/5-mm thick. Twist into pretzel shapes by making a circle, then twist the ends through each other to form a letter "B." Place on the baking sheet, allowing room for expansion during cooking.

3 Bake in the hot oven for 8–12 minutes. Let cool slightly on the baking sheet, then transfer to a wire rack to cool completely.

4 Melt the butter and chocolate in a bowl set over a pan of gently simmering water, stirring to blend. Dip half of each pretzel into the chocolate and allow the excess chocolate to drip back into the bowl. Place the pretzels on a sheet of parchment paper and let set. When set, dust the non-chocolate coated side of each pretzel with confectioners' sugar before serving.

chocolate wheatmeals

makes 20

prep: 10 mins, plus ⟲
50 mins cooling/setting

cook: 25 mins ⟲

A good everyday cookie, these wheatmeals will keep well in an airtight container for at least 1 week. Dip in white, milk, or semisweet chocolate and serve as a tasty mid-morning snack.

INGREDIENTS

6 tbsp butter, plus extra for greasing

½ cup raw demerara sugar

1 egg

¼ cup wheat germ

scant 1 cup whole-wheat flour

6 tbsp self rising flour, sifted

4½ oz/125 g chocolate

---

variation

If you like, add scant ⅜ cup chopped mixed nuts to the mixture in Step 1 and proceed as in main recipe.

---

cook's tip

These cookies can be frozen very successfully. Freeze them at the end of Step 3 for up to 3 months. Thaw and then dip them in melted chocolate.

1 Preheat the oven to 350°F/180°C. Grease a baking sheet. Beat the butter and sugar until fluffy. Add the egg and beat well. Stir in the wheat germ and flours. Bring the batter together with your hands.

2 Roll rounded teaspoons of the batter into balls and place

on the prepared baking sheet, allowing room for expansion during cooking.

3 Flatten the cookies slightly with a fork, then bake in the preheated oven for 15–20 minutes, or until golden. Let cool on the baking sheet for a few minutes before transferring to a wire rack to cool completely.

4 Melt the chocolate (see pages 9–10), then dip each cookie in the chocolate to cover the bases and come a little way up the sides. Let the excess chocolate drip back into the bowl. Place the cookies on a sheet of parchment paper and let set in a cool place before serving.

chocolate orange cookies

⏲ **cook: 10–12 mins**   ⏱ **prep: 15 mins, plus
50 mins cooling/setting**   **makes 30**

*These delicious chocolate cookies have a tangy orange frosting.
Children love them, especially if different shaped cutters are used.*

---

variation

You can also make chocolate lemon
cookies. Replace the orange juice
with lemon juice.

---

cook's tip

You can buy a variety of cookie
cutters from kitchen stores. They are
sold individually or as sets and are
available in different sizes and
shapes. For this recipe use a fluted
round cutter.

INGREDIENTS

6 tbsp butter, softened

6 tbsp superfine sugar

1 egg

1 tbsp milk

1½ cups all-purpose flour, plus
extra for dusting

2 tbsp unsweetened cocoa

FROSTING

1⅓ cups confectioners' sugar, sifted

3 tbsp orange juice

1 oz/25 g semisweet chocolate, melted
(see pages 9–10)

1 Preheat the oven to
350°F/180°C. Line
2 baking sheets with sheets
of parchment paper.

2 Beat the butter and
sugar together until
light and fluffy. Beat in the egg
and milk until well blended.
Sift the flour and cocoa
together and gradually mix
together to form a soft dough.

Use your fingers to incorporate
the last of the flour and bring
the dough together.

3 Roll out the dough on
a lightly floured counter
until ¼-inch/5-mm thick. Using
a 2-inch/5-cm fluted round
cutter, cut out as many cookies
as you can. Re-roll the dough
trimmings and cut out more
cookies. Place the cookies on

the prepared baking sheet,
allowing room for expansion
during cooking and bake in the
hot oven for 10–12 minutes, or
until golden brown.

4 Let the cookies cool
on the baking sheet
for a few minutes, then
transfer to a wire rack and
let cool completely.

5 To make the frosting,
place the confectioners'
sugar in a bowl and stir in
enough orange juice to form
a thin frosting that will coat
the back of a spoon. Spread
the frosting over the cookies
and let set. Drizzle with
melted chocolate. Let set
before serving.

mocha walnut cookies

makes about 16 **prep: 20 mins, plus 20 mins cooling** **cook: 10–15 mins**

These cookies have a lovely chewy texture and make a wonderful afternoon treat. They are also ideal for birthday parties.

INGREDIENTS

4 oz/115 g butter, softened, plus extra for greasing

½ cup firmly packed light brown sugar

⅜ cup golden granulated sugar

1 tsp vanilla extract

1 tbsp instant coffee granules, dissolved in 1 tbsp hot water

1 cup all-purpose flour

½ tsp baking powder

¼ tsp baking soda

⅓ cup milk chocolate chips

¼ cup shelled walnuts, coarsely chopped

cook's tip

Brown sugar has a tendency to be quite lumpy, so it is a good idea to sift it before use when baking cakes and cookies.

1. Preheat the oven to 350°F/180°C. Grease 2 baking sheets with butter. Place the butter, brown sugar, and granulated sugar in a large mixing bowl and beat together thoroughly until light and fluffy. Place the vanilla extract, coffee, and egg in a separate bowl and whisk together.

2. Gradually add the coffee mixture to the butter and sugar, beating until fluffy. Sift the flour, baking powder, and baking soda into the cookie batter and fold in carefully. Fold in the chocolate chips and walnuts.

3. Place dessertspoonfuls of the cookie batter onto the prepared baking sheets, allowing room for the cookies to spread. Bake in the oven for 10–15 minutes, or until crisp on the outside but still soft inside. Let cool on the baking sheets for 2 minutes, then transfer to wire racks to cool completely.

chocolate viennese fingers

⏲ **cook: 15 mins**

⏱ **prep: 20 mins, plus
40 mins cooling/setting**

makes about 30

*These melt-in-the-mouth cookies are ideal served with coffee or as
an accompaniment to fruit fools and mousses.*

cook's tip

Sprinkle some chopped nuts onto
the chocolate-coated ends of these
cookies while the chocolate is still
soft, if you like.

INGREDIENTS

4 oz/115 g butter, softened, plus
extra for greasing

½ cup golden confectioners'
sugar, sifted

generous ¾ cup all-purpose flour

1 tbsp unsweetened cocoa

3½ oz/100 g semisweet chocolate,
melted and cooled (see pages 9–10)

1 Preheat the oven
to 350°F/180°C. Grease
2 baking sheets. Beat the
butter and sugar together until
light and fluffy. Sift the flour
and unsweetened cocoa into
the bowl and work the
mixture until it is a smooth,
piping consistency.

2 Spoon into a large
pastry bag fitted with
a 1-inch/2.5-cm fluted tip. Pipe
2½-inch/6-cm lengths of the
mixture onto the prepared
baking sheets, allowing room
for expansion during cooking.
Bake in the preheated oven for
15 minutes, or until firm.

3 Let cool on the baking
sheets for 2 minutes,
then transfer to a wire rack to
cool completely. Dip the ends
of the cookies into the
melted chocolate and let set
before serving.

lebkuchen

makes about 60

**prep: 20 mins, plus ⏲
40 mins cooling/setting**

cook: 20–25 mins

*These little spicy cookies are traditionally eaten in Germany on
St Nicholas Day, 6 December, but they are great to eat at any time
of the year. Serve with freshly brewed coffee.*

INGREDIENTS

3 eggs

1 cup golden superfine sugar

scant ½ cup all-purpose flour

2 tsp unsweetened cocoa

1 tsp ground cinnamon

½ tsp ground cardamom

¼ tsp ground cloves

¼ tsp ground nutmeg

1½ cups ground almonds

⅓ cup candied peel, finely chopped

TO DECORATE

**4 oz/115 g semisweet chocolate,
melted and cooled (see pages 9–10)**

**4 oz/115 g white chocolate,
melted and cooled (see pages 9–10)**

sugar crystals

variation

Instead of sprinkling sugar crystals
over the finished cookies, replace
with sifted confectioners' sugar.

cook's tip

After dipping the cookies in melted
chocolate in Step 3, you can leave
them to set on waxed paper to catch
any drips. Store the cookies in an
airtight container for up to 3 days.

1 Preheat the oven
to 325°F/160°C. Line
several baking sheets with
nonstick parchment paper.
Place the eggs and sugar in a
small heatproof bowl and set
over a pan of gently simmering
water. Whisk until thick and
foamy. Remove the bowl from
the pan and continue to whisk
for 2 minutes.

2 Sift the flour, cocoa,
cinnamon, cardamom,
cloves, and nutmeg over the
egg mixture, add the ground
almonds and chopped peel
and stir. Drop heaping
teaspoonfuls of the cookie
batter onto the prepared
baking sheets, spreading them
gently into smooth mounds
and allowing room for
expansion during cooking.

3 Bake in the oven for
15–20 minutes, or until
light brown and slightly soft
to the touch. Let cool on the
baking sheets for 10 minutes,
then transfer to wire racks to
cool completely. Dip half the
cookies in the melted
semisweet chocolate and
half in the white chocolate.
Sprinkle with sugar crystals,
let set, then serve.

dutch macaroons

⏱ **cook: 25 mins**   ⏲ **prep: 10 mins, plus 40 mins cooling/setting**   **makes 20**

These unusual cookie treats are delicious served with coffee.
They also make an ideal dessert cookie to serve with ice cream.

variation

Instead of using semisweet chocolate, melt 1 oz/25 g white chocolate (see pages 9–10) and drizzle over the top of the cookies.

cook's tip

Rice paper is edible so you can just break off the excess from round the edge of the cookies. Remove it completely before dipping in the chocolate, if you prefer.

INGREDIENTS

rice paper

2 egg whites

generous 1 cup superfine sugar

generous 1⅔ cups ground almonds

8 oz/225 g semisweet chocolate

1 Preheat the oven to 350°F/180°C. Cover 2 baking sheets with rice paper. Whisk the egg whites in a large, clean bowl until stiff, then fold in the sugar and ground almonds.

2 Place the mixture in a large pastry bag fitted with a ½-inch/1-cm plain tip

and pipe fingers, 3-inches/ 7.5-cm long, allowing room for expansion during cooking.

3 Bake in the hot oven for 15–20 minutes, or until golden. Transfer to a wire rack and let cool. Remove the excess rice paper from round the edges.

4 Melt the chocolate (see pages 9–10) and dip the base of each cookie into the chocolate. Place the macaroons on a sheet of parchment paper and let set. Drizzle any remaining chocolate over the top of the cookies (you may have to reheat the chocolate in order to do this). Let set before serving.

chocolate & nut crescents

makes about 40

prep: 20 mins, plus 20 mins cooling

cook: 20–25 mins

These crisp little cookies are a variation on a cookie that is served in Greece for festivals and special occasions.

INGREDIENTS

8 oz/225 g butter, softened,
plus extra for greasing

⅜ cup golden superfine sugar

1 egg yolk

1 tsp rum

½ cup shelled walnuts, ground

generous 1½ cups all-purpose flour,
plus extra for shaping

⅜ cup cornstarch

1 tbsp unsweetened cocoa

¾ cup confectioners' sugar, sifted,
to coat

variation

For an Italian flavor, replace the rum with 1 tsp of amaretto liqueur and the walnuts with 1 cup almonds ground in a food processor.

1 Preheat the oven to 350°F/180°C. Grease several baking sheets. Place the butter and sugar in a bowl and beat together until pale and fluffy. Beat in the egg yolk and rum. Stir in the walnuts. Sift the flour, cornstarch, and unsweetened cocoa over the mixture and stir, adding a little more flour, if necessary, to make a firm dough.

2 With lightly floured hands, break off walnut-size pieces of dough and roll into 3-inch/7.5-cm lengths, thick in the center and tapering into pointed ends. Shape into crescents and place on the prepared baking sheets.

3 Bake in the oven for 20–25 minutes, or until firm. Let cool on the baking sheets for 2 minutes, then transfer to wire racks to cool completely. Before serving, gently toss the cookies in a little sifted confectioners' sugar, to coat completely.

nutty chocolate & orange curls

cook: 8–10 mins

prep: 15 mins, plus 15 mins cooling

makes 18

These wafer-thin, crisp, nutty cookies are ideal for serving with fresh fruit desserts or vanilla ice cream.

cook's tip

Do not be tempted to bake more than one sheet of cookies at a time, otherwise the second batch will become too firm before you have had time to shape them.

INGREDIENTS

2 oz/55 g butter, melted and cooled, plus extra for greasing

2 egg whites

scant ⅔ cup golden superfine sugar

⅓ cup all-purpose flour

1 tbsp unsweetened cocoa

¼ cup slivered almonds

grated rind of 1 orange

1 Preheat the oven to 350°F/180°C. Grease 2 or 3 baking sheets and a rolling pin with butter. Place the egg whites and sugar in a bowl. Whisk together with a fork until frothy. Sift the flour and unsweetened cocoa into the bowl. Add the almonds and orange rind and mix with a fork. Add the butter and mix together.

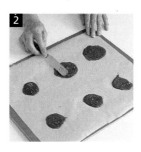

2 Drop teaspoonfuls of the cookie batter onto the prepared baking sheets, allowing plenty of room for expansion during cooking. Using a spatula, spread each one out slightly. Bake in the preheated oven, one baking sheet at a time, for 8–10 minutes, or until the edges of the cookies are firm to the touch.

3 Carefully remove the cookies with a spatula and place over the prepared rolling pin while still warm. Let stand for 1–2 minutes, or until set, then carefully remove and transfer to a wire rack to cool. Store in an airtight container.

hazelnut & chocolate oat crunch bars

makes 12 **prep: 10 mins, plus 30 mins cooling** **cook: 25–30 mins**

These chewy, nutty oat crunch bars are very filling, so they are great for tucking into a lunch box for a sustaining snack on the move.

INGREDIENTS

4 oz/115 g butter, plus extra for greasing

2⅓ cups rolled oats

⅜ cup shelled hazelnuts, lightly toasted and chopped

scant ½ cup all-purpose flour

⅜ cup light brown sugar

2 tbsp corn syrup

½ cup semisweet chocolate chips

variation

For a special treat, melt 4 oz/115 g semisweet chocolate (see pages 9–10) and spread over the top of the oat crunch bars. Let set before serving.

1 Preheat the oven to 350°F/180°C. Grease a 9-inch/23-cm shallow square pan with butter. Place the oats, hazelnuts, and flour in a large bowl and mix.

2 Place the butter, sugar, and syrup in a pan and heat gently until the sugar has dissolved. Pour onto the dry ingredients and mix well. Stir in the chocolate chips.

3 Turn the mixture into the prepared pan and bake in the preheated oven for 20–25 minutes, or until golden brown and firm to the touch. Mark into 12 rectangles using a knife and let cool in the pan. Cut the oat crunch bars with a sharp knife, remove from the pan, and serve.

chocolate & vanilla pinwheels

cook: 10–15 mins   **prep: 20 mins, plus 1 hr 20 mins chilling/cooling**   **makes about 36**

These crisp little cookies are a variation on a cookie that is served in Greece for festivals and special occasions.

variation

For a different look, in Step 3, place the vanilla dough on waxed paper, then place the chocolate dough on top.

INGREDIENTS

8 oz/225 g butter, softened, plus extra for greasing

scant ⅔ cup golden superfine sugar

2⅓ cups all-purpose flour, plus extra for dusting

1 tbsp unsweetened cocoa

1 tsp vanilla extract

1 Grease 2 or 3 baking sheets with butter. Beat the butter and sugar together until light and fluffy. Transfer half the mixture to a separate bowl and add generous 1 cup of the flour and all of the cocoa. Stir the vanilla extract into the other half of the mixture. Sift in the remaining flour. Stir both mixtures to make firm, pliable doughs.

2 Roll out each piece of dough on a floured counter into a rectangle measuring 8 x 11 inches/ 20 x 28 cm. Place the chocolate dough on a large sheet of waxed paper and carefully place the vanilla dough on top. Roll up firmly from one long side, using the paper to guide the rolling. Wrap the roll in the paper and

let chill in the refrigerator for at least 1 hour, or until the dough is firm.

3 Preheat the oven to 350°F/180°C. Unwrap the dough and cut into thin slices. Place the cookies on the prepared baking sheets and bake in the oven for 10–15 minutes, or until golden. Let cool on the

baking sheets for 2 minutes, then transfer to wire racks to cool completely before serving.

chocolate chip shortbread

serves 8

prep: 10 mins, plus ⏲
30 mins cooling

cook: 35–40 mins ⏲

Buttery shortbread sprinkled with chocolate chips—nothing could be simpler and more delicious!

INGREDIENTS

4 oz/115 g butter, diced, plus extra
for greasing

generous ¾ cup all-purpose flour

⅜ cup cornstarch

generous ¼ cup golden superfine sugar

¼ cup semisweet chocolate chips

---

variation

To give the shortbread a crunchier texture, use semolina as a substitute for the cornstarch. Use milk or white chocolate chips in place of semisweet.

1 Preheat the oven to 325°F/160°C. Grease a 9-inch/23-cm loose-bottom fluted tart pan with butter. Sift the flour and cornstarch into a large mixing bowl. Stir in the sugar, then add the butter and rub it in until the mixture starts to bind together.

2 Turn into the prepared tart pan and press evenly over the base. Prick the surface with a fork. Sprinkle with the chocolate chips and press lightly into the surface.

3 Bake in the oven for 35–40 minutes, or until cooked but not browned.

Mark into 8 portions with a sharp knife. Let cool in the pan for 10 minutes, then transfer to a wire rack to cool completely.

cookies & cream sandwiches

cook: 20 mins **prep: 25 mins, plus 2 hrs 20 mins cooling/chilling** **makes 12**

Delicious chocolate shortbread cookies, with a hint of spice, are sandwiched together with chocolate cream.

cook's tip

Do not sandwich the cookies together too long before serving, otherwise they will go soft. Store unsandwiched cookies in an airtight container for up to 3 days.

INGREDIENTS

4½ oz/125 g butter, softened

scant ¾ cup golden confectioners' sugar

scant 1 cup all-purpose flour

⅜ cup unsweetened cocoa

½ tsp ground cinnamon

FILLING

4½ oz/125 g semisweet chocolate, broken into pieces

¼ cup heavy cream

1 Preheat the oven to 325°F/160°C. Line a baking sheet with nonstick parchment paper. Place the butter and sugar in a large bowl and beat together until light and fluffy. Sift the flour, unsweetened cocoa, and ground cinnamon into the bowl and mix until a smooth dough forms.

2 Place the dough between 2 sheets of nonstick parchment paper and roll out to ⅛-inch/3-mm thick. Cut out 2½-inch/6-cm circles and place on the prepared baking sheet. Bake in the oven for 15 minutes, or until firm to the touch. Let cool for 2 minutes, then transfer to wire racks to cool completely.

3 Meanwhile, make the filling. Place the chocolate and cream in a pan and heat gently until the chocolate has melted. Stir until smooth. Let cool, then let chill in the refrigerator for 2 hours, or until firm. Sandwich the cookies together in pairs with a spoonful of chocolate cream and serve.

pineapple & cherry florentines

makes about 14 **prep: 15 mins, plus 2 hrs** ↺ **cooling/setting** **cook: 10–12 mins** ⏱

Florentines are a lovely combination of fruit and nuts in a delicate crisp cookie with a chocolate coating. They are good for serving with vanilla ice cream and also make a welcome gift.

INGREDIENTS

2 oz/55 g butter

scant ¼ cup raw brown sugar

1 tbsp corn syrup

⅜ cup all-purpose flour, sifted

2 tbsp angelica, coarsely chopped

⅛ cup candied cherries, coarsely chopped

½ cup slivered almonds, coarsely chopped

¼ cup candied pineapple, coarsely chopped

1 tsp lemon juice

4 oz/115 g semisweet chocolate, melted and cooled (see pages 9–10)

---

variation

White chocolate can be used instead of semisweet. They look attractive if half are coated with semisweet chocolate and half with white.

---

cook's tip

If you have difficulty removing the florentines from the baking sheet, return to the oven for 2 minutes, then lift off and let cool on a wire rack.

1 Preheat the oven to 350°F/180°C. Line several baking sheets with nonstick parchment paper. Place the butter, sugar, and syrup in a pan and heat gently until melted, then stir in the flour, angelica, cherries, almonds, pineapple, and lemon juice.

2 Place walnut-size mounds of the mixture well apart on the baking sheets and flatten with a fork. Bake in the oven for 8–10 minutes, or until golden. Use a spatula to neaten the ragged edges. Let cool for 1 minute, then transfer to a wire rack to cool completely.

3 Spread the melted chocolate over the base of each florentine, placing the cookies, chocolate side up, on a wire rack. Use a fork to mark the chocolate into wavy lines. Let stand until set.

ladies' kisses

makes 20 **prep: 30 mins, plus 2 hrs** ⟳ **cook: 30 mins**
30 mins chilling/cooling

*These tiny cookies sandwiched together with melted chocolate are
lovely at teatime or served as petits fours after dinner.*

INGREDIENTS

5 oz/140 g unsalted butter

generous ½ cup superfine sugar

1 egg yolk

generous 1 cup ground almonds

generous 1 cup all-purpose flour

2 oz/55 g semisweet chocolate,
broken into pieces

2 tbsp confectioners' sugar

2 tbsp unsweetened cocoa

variation

Replace the semisweet chocolate with
the same amount of white chocolate.
Omit the confectioners' sugar and use
4 tablespoons cocoa for dusting.

cook's tip

Place the dough balls well apart
from each other on the baking
sheets as they will spread out during
cooking. You may need to cook the
cookies in batches.

1 Line 3 baking trays
with parchment paper,
or use 3 nonstick sheets. Beat
the butter and sugar together
in a bowl until pale and fluffy.
Beat in the egg yolk, then beat
in the almonds and flour.
Continue beating until well
mixed. Shape the dough into
a ball, wrap in plastic wrap,
and let chill in the refrigerator
for 1½–2 hours.

2 Preheat the oven
to 325°F/160°C.
Unwrap the dough, break off
walnut-size pieces, and roll
them into balls between the
palms of your hands. Place the
dough balls on the prepared
baking sheets, allowing room
for expansion during cooking.
Bake in the preheated oven for
20–25 minutes, or until golden
brown. Carefully transfer the

cookies, still on the parchment
paper, if using, to wire racks
to cool.

3 Place the semisweet
chocolate in a small
heatproof bowl and set over
a pan of barely simmering
water, stirring constantly, until
melted. Remove the bowl from
the heat.

4 Remove the cookies
from the parchment
paper, if using, and spread the
melted chocolate over the
bases. Sandwich them together
in pairs and return to the wire
racks to cool. Dust with a
mixture of confectioners' sugar
and cocoa and serve.

tiffin

cook: 5 mins

prep: 10 mins, plus 9 hrs 30 mins soaking/chilling

makes 12 pieces

Tiffin is a wonderful uncooked cookie cake containing semisweet chocolate, dried fruit, and nuts. You can cut it into smaller pieces to serve with after-dinner coffee.

variation

If this is to be served to children, use orange juice instead of brandy for soaking the raisins.

cook's tip

For a decorative effect, use a fork to lightly mark wavy lines over the chocolate topping before letting it set in the refrigerator overnight.

INGREDIENTS

⅓ cup raisins

2 tbsp brandy

4 oz/115 g semisweet chocolate, broken into pieces

4 oz/115 g milk chocolate, broken into pieces

2 oz/55 g butter, plus extra for greasing

2 tbsp corn syrup

6 oz/175 g graham crackers, coarsely broken

½ cup slivered almonds, lightly toasted

⅛ cup candied cherries, chopped

TOPPING

3½ oz/100 g semisweet chocolate, broken into pieces

¾ oz/20 g butter

1 Grease and line the bottom of a 7-inch/ 18-cm shallow square pan. Place the raisins and brandy in a bowl and let soak for 30 minutes. Put the chocolate, butter, and syrup in a pan and heat gently until melted.

2 Stir in the graham crackers, almonds, cherries, raisins, and brandy.

Turn into the prepared pan and let cool. Cover and let chill in the refrigerator for 1 hour.

3 To make the topping, place the chocolate and butter in a small heatproof bowl and set over a pan of gently simmering water until melted. Stir and pour the chocolate mixture over the cookie base. Let chill in the

refrigerator for 8 hours, or overnight. Cut into bars or squares to serve.

no-bake chocolate squares

makes 16

prep: 10 mins, plus 2 hrs 20 mins chilling/setting

cook: 5 mins

Children will enjoy making these as an introduction to chocolate cooking, and they keep well in the refrigerator.

INGREDIENTS

9½ oz/275 g semisweet chocolate

6 oz/175 g butter

4 tbsp golden syrup

2 tbsp dark rum (optional)

6 oz/175 g plain cookies

⅓ cup toasted rice cereal

generous ¼ cup chopped walnuts or pecans

generous ½ cup candied cherries, coarsely chopped

1 oz/25 g white chocolate, to decorate

---

variation

Brandy or an orange-flavored liqueur can be used instead of the rum, if you prefer. Cherry brandy also works well.

1 Line a 7-inch/18-cm square cake pan with parchment paper. Place the semisweet chocolate in a large bowl with the butter, syrup, and rum, if using, and set over a pan of gently simmering water until melted, stirring constantly, until blended.

2 Break the cookies into small pieces and stir into the chocolate mixture with the rice cereal, nuts, and cherries.

3 Pour the batter into the pan and level the top, pressing down well with the back of a spoon. Let chill in the refrigerator for 2 hours.

4 To decorate, melt the white chocolate (see pages 9–10) and drizzle it over the top of the cake in a random pattern. Let set. To serve, carefully turn out of the pan and remove the parchment paper. Cut into 16 squares and serve.

caramel chocolate shortbread

makes 24   **prep: 10 mins, plus 1 hr chilling/setting**   **cook: 30 mins**

This is a truly luxurious shortbread, combined with a sumptuous layer of caramel topped with crisp chocolate.

INGREDIENTS

4 oz/115 g butter, plus extra for greasing

generous 1 cup all-purpose flour

generous ¼ cup golden superfine sugar

7 oz/200 g semisweet chocolate, broken into pieces

CARAMEL

6 oz/175 g butter

generous ½ cup golden superfine sugar

3 tbsp corn syrup

14 oz/400 g canned condensed milk

variation

A white chocolate topping will also work. Replace the semisweet chocolate with the same amount of white.

cook's tip

Take great care when cooking the caramel filling as it can easily catch and burn on the bottom of the pan. Keep stirring until thick, then remove from the heat immediately.

1 Preheat the oven to 350°F/180°C. Grease and line the bottom of a 9-inch/23-cm shallow square cake pan. Place the butter, flour, and sugar in a food processor and process until it starts to bind together. Press into the pan and level the top. Bake in the preheated oven for 20–25 minutes, or until golden.

2 Meanwhile, make the caramel. Place the butter, sugar, syrup, and condensed milk in a heavy-bottom pan. Heat gently until the sugar has melted. Bring to a boil, then reduce the heat and let simmer for 6–8 minutes, stirring, until very thick. Pour over the shortbread and let chill in the refrigerator for 2 hours, or until firm.

3 Melt the chocolate (see pages 9–10) and let cool, then spread over the caramel. Let chill in the refrigerator for 2 hours, or until set. Cut the shortbread into 12 pieces using a sharp knife and serve.

chocolate crispy bites

⏲ cook: 10 mins   ⏱ prep: 45 mins, plus   makes 16
                            2 hrs chilling

A favorite with children, this version of crispy bites has been given a new twist, which is sure to be very popular.

variation
For a change, place a spoonful of the white chocolate batter in paper cake cases and top with a spoonful of the semisweet chocolate. Chill until hard.

INGREDIENTS

WHITE LAYER	DARK LAYER
4 tbsp butter, plus extra for greasing	4 tbsp butter
1 tbsp corn syrup	2 tbsp corn syrup
5½ oz/150 g white chocolate, broken into small pieces	4½ oz/125 g semisweet chocolate, broken into small pieces
generous ½ cup toasted rice cereal	scant 1 cup toasted rice cereal

cook's tip
These crispy bites can be made up to 4 days ahead. Keep them covered in the refrigerator until ready to use, then cut into small squares and serve.

1 Grease an 8-inch/20-cm square cake pan and line with parchment paper. To make the white chocolate layer, place the butter, syrup, and chocolate in a heatproof bowl and set over a pan of gently simmering water until melted. Remove from the heat and stir in the rice cereal until well blended. Press into the pan and level the surface.

2 To make the dark chocolate layer, place the butter, syrup, and semisweet chocolate in a heatproof bowl and set over a pan of gently simmering water until melted.

3 Remove the pan from the heat and stir in the rice cereal until well blended. Pour the dark chocolate layer over the white chocolate layer, and let chill in the refrigerator for 2 hours, or until hardened. Turn out of the cake pan and cut into small squares, using a sharp knife.

panforte di siena

serves 12–16   **prep: 10 mins, plus 20 mins cooling**   **cook: 35–40 mins**

Chewy, sticky panforte is the traditional Christmas cake of Siena. Chocolate was first added to the recipe when cocoa arrived from the New World and became the fashionable ingredient.

INGREDIENTS

butter, for greasing
¼ cup candied cherries, quartered
⅔ cup mixed candied orange and lemon peel, finely chopped
2 tbsp candied ginger, coarsely chopped
1 cup slivered almonds
¾ cup hazelnuts, toasted and coarsely ground
⅜ cup all-purpose flour

¼ cup unsweetened cocoa
1 tsp ground cinnamon
¼ tsp ground cloves
¼ tsp ground nutmeg
¼ tsp ground coriander
½ cup honey
generous ½ cup golden superfine sugar
1 tsp orange flower water
confectioners' sugar, for dusting

variation

You can replace the candied cherries with dried cranberries and the candied ginger with the same amount of candied pineapple.

cook's tip

Panforte will keep in an airtight container for up to 2 months. Do not store it in a plastic container, otherwise the panforte may taste musty. Sift with confectioners' sugar before serving.

1 Preheat the oven to 325°F/160°C. Thoroughly grease the bottom of an 8-inch/20-cm loose-bottom cake or tart pan. Line the bottom with nonstick parchment paper. Place the cherries, candied peel, ginger, almonds, and hazelnuts in a bowl. Sift in the flour, cocoa, cinnamon, cloves, nutmeg, and coriander, and mix. Set aside.

2 Place the honey, sugar, and orange flower water in a pan and heat gently until the sugar has dissolved. Bring the mixture to a boil and boil steadily until a temperature of 241°F/116°C has been reached on a sugar thermometer, or a small amount of the mixture forms a soft ball when dropped into cold water.

3 Quickly remove the pan from the heat and stir in the dry ingredients. Mix thoroughly and turn into the prepared pan. Spread evenly and bake in the preheated oven for 30 minutes. Let cool in the pan. Turn out and carefully peel away the lining paper. Dust confectioners' sugar lightly over the top and cut into wedges to serve.

candies & drinks

It is surprising just how easy candies are to make at home, and how delicious! They will always bring a touch of luxury and sophistication to a dinner party, and the fact that they can be made in advance is an added bonus when entertaining. Try the decorative Chocolate Orange Collettes (see page 231) or the irresistible Chocolate-Dipped Fruit (see page 240), which makes an ideal light alternative to a traditional festive dessert. Homemade chocolates, attractively packaged, also make much-appreciated Christmas and birthday gifts. Irish Cream Truffles (see page 234) are extravagantly rich, while Pecan Mocha Fudge (see page 237) will delight the fudge-lover in your family.

Chocolate lends itself particularly well to warming drinks, and mixes deliciously with a whole variety of liqueurs and spirits. Mexicana (see page 250) is an ambrosial combination of coffee, chocolate, and whipped cream, while Café Mocha (see page 253) is set off seductively with coffee-flavored ice cream. Children will love the Quick Chocolate Milk Shake (see page 248)—even the reluctant milk-drinkers!

chocolate orange collettes

cook: 5–10 mins

**prep: 40 mins, plus
2 hrs chilling**

makes 20

*Delicate chocolate cases filled with a soft, deliciously rich
truffle mixture look as good as they taste.*

variation

Make some or all of the chocolate
cases with white chocolate, or use
white chocolate in some or all of the
filling, if you like.

cook's tip

To get fine strips of orange rind,
either use a zester or cut into thin
strips with a vegetable peeler and
shred into fine strips.

INGREDIENTS

10 oz/280 g semisweet chocolate,
broken into pieces

½ tsp corn oil

⅔ cup heavy cream

finely grated rind of ½ orange

1 tbsp Cointreau

TO DECORATE

chopped nuts

fine strips of orange rind

1 Melt 5½ oz/150 g of
the chocolate with the
oil (see pages 9–10) and stir
until mixed. Spread evenly over
the inside of 20 double petit
four cases, taking care to keep
a good thickness round the
edge. Let chill for 1 hour, or
until set, then apply a second
coat of chocolate, remelting if
necessary. Let chill for 1 hour,
or until completely set.

2 Place the cream and
grated orange rind in
a pan and heat until almost
boiling. Remove from the heat,
add the remaining chocolate
pieces and stir until smooth.
Return to the heat and stir
until the mixture starts to
bubble. Remove from the heat
and stir in the Cointreau. Let
cool. Peel the paper cases off
the chocolate cups.

3 Beat the chocolate
cream until thick, then
spoon into a large pastry bag
fitted with a fluted tip. Pipe
the chocolate cream into the
chocolate cases. Decorate
some of the chocolate collettes
with chopped nuts and some
with a few strips of orange
rind. Cover and keep in the
refrigerator. Use within
2–3 days.

rum & chocolate cups

serves 12   **prep: 25 mins, plus 2 hrs** ⏱ **chilling/cooling**   **cook: 10–15 mins** ⏱

Use firm foil confectionery cases, rather than paper ones, to make the chocolate cups, because they offer extra support.

INGREDIENTS

2 oz/55 g semisweet chocolate, broken into pieces

12 toasted hazelnuts

FILLING

4 oz/115 g semisweet chocolate, broken into pieces

1 tbsp dark rum

4 tbsp mascarpone cheese

variation

For a change, replace the semisweet chocolate in the filling for the same amount of white chocolate.

cook's tip

When melting the chocolate in Step 1, stir the chocolate thoroughly until it is melted and smooth, but not too runny, otherwise it will be difficult to coat the cases.

1 To make the chocolate cups, place the semisweet chocolate in the top of a double boiler or in a heatproof bowl set over a pan of barely simmering water. Stir over low heat until the chocolate is just melted but not too runny, then remove from the heat. Spoon ½ teaspoon of melted chocolate into a foil confectionery case and brush it over the base and up the sides. Coat 11 more foil cases in the same way and let set for 30 minutes. Let chill in the refrigerator for 15 minutes. If necessary, reheat the chocolate in the double boiler or heatproof bowl to melt it again, then coat the foil cases with a second, slightly thinner coating. Chill in the refrigerator for an additional 30 minutes.

2 To make the filling, place the chocolate in the top of a double boiler or in a heatproof bowl set over a pan of barely simmering water. Stir over low heat until melted and smooth, then remove from the heat. Let cool slightly, stir in the rum, and beat in the mascarpone cheese until smooth. Let cool completely, stirring occasionally.

3 Spoon the filling into a pastry bag fitted with a ½-inch/1-cm star tip. Carefully peel away the confectionery cases from the chocolate cups. Pipe the filling into the cups and top each one with a toasted hazelnut.

irish cream truffles

makes about 24

prep: 35 mins, plus 10–12 hrs chilling

cook: 5–10 mins

Truffles are simple to make and will impress your guests at the end of a dinner party. They are also the ideal gift for chocoholics.

INGREDIENTS

⅔ cup heavy cream

8 oz/225 g semisweet chocolate, broken into pieces

1 oz/25 g butter

3 tbsp Irish cream liqueur

4 oz/115 g white chocolate, broken into pieces

4 oz/115 g semisweet chocolate, broken into pieces

variation

Brandy, rum, or Grand Marnier can be used instead of Irish cream liqueur. After coating the truffles in chocolate, roll them in chopped nuts.

cook's tip

If the truffle mixture is too firm to roll into small balls when it comes out of the refrigerator, let it soften at room temperature for a few minutes.

1 Heat the cream in a pan over low heat but do not let it boil. Remove from the heat and stir in the chocolate and butter. Let stand for 2 minutes, then stir until smooth. Stir in the liqueur. Pour the mixture into a bowl and let cool. Cover and let chill in the refrigerator for 8 hours, or overnight, until firm.

2 Line a baking sheet with nonstick parchment paper. Take teaspoonfuls of the chilled chocolate mixture and roll into small balls. Place the balls on the prepared baking sheet and let chill in the refrigerator for 2–4 hours, or until firm. Melt the white chocolate pieces (see pages 9–10) and let cool slightly.

3 Coat half the truffles by spearing on thin skewers or toothpicks and dipping into the white chocolate. Transfer to a sheet of nonstick parchment paper to set. Melt the semisweet chocolate and let cool slightly, then use to coat the remaining truffles in the same way. Store the truffles in the refrigerator in an airtight container, separated by layers of waxed paper, for up to 1 week.

white chocolate & pistachio truffles

 cook: 5 mins

 prep: 30 mins, plus
10 hrs chilling

makes 26–30

*These wickedly rich truffles add a touch of decadence to the end of
a light meal. They look attractive arranged in a glass serving dish.*

variation

Use ready-flavored chocolate, such
as coffee or orange, combined
with chopped hazelnuts, walnuts,
or almonds.

cook's tip

The truffles look best if they are quite
rough, rather than being rolled into
smooth balls. Roll the truffles lightly
in the icing sugar, otherwise they will
taste very sweet.

INGREDIENTS

3½ oz/100 g white chocolate,
broken into pieces

½ oz/15 g butter

generous ¼ cup heavy cream

⅛ cup shelled unsalted pistachios,
finely chopped

confectioners' sugar, for coating

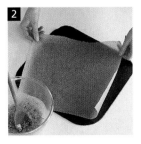

1 Place the chocolate,
butter, and cream in a
heatproof bowl and set over a
pan of gently simmering water
until melted, without stirring.
Remove the bowl from the
heat and stir gently, then stir in
the nuts. Let cool, then cover
with plastic wrap and let chill
in the refrigerator for 8 hours,
or overnight.

2 Line a baking sheet
with nonstick
parchment paper. Take
teaspoonfuls of the mixture
and roll into balls. Place the
truffles on the prepared baking
sheet and let chill for 2 hours,
or until firm.

3 Just before serving,
roll the truffles in
confectioners' sugar to coat.

pecan mocha fudge

cook: 15–20 mins   **prep: 15 mins, plus 2 hrs setting**   makes 80 pieces

This recipe makes plenty of delicious fudge for eating yourself, for sharing and for giving away as presents!

variation

Chopped unsalted pistachios, Brazil nuts, almonds, or walnuts can be used instead of the pecans.

cook's tip

To test the temperature of the fudge accurately, it is best to use a sugar thermometer. These are available from specialist kitchenware stores.

INGREDIENTS

1¼ cups milk

2 lb 4 oz/1 kg golden granulated sugar

9 oz/250 g butter, plus extra

for greasing

2 tbsp instant coffee granules

2 tbsp unsweetened cocoa

2 tbsp corn syrup

14 oz/400 g canned condensed milk

½ cup shelled pecans, chopped

1 Grease a 12 x 9-inch/ 30 x 23-cm jelly roll pan. Place the milk, sugar, and butter in a large pan. Stir over gentle heat until the sugar has dissolved. Stir in the coffee granules, unsweetened cocoa, syrup, and condensed milk.

2 Bring to a boil and boil steadily, whisking constantly, for 10 minutes, or until a temperature of 241°F/116°C has been reached on a sugar thermometer, or a small amount of the mixture forms a soft ball when dropped into cold water.

3 Let cool for 5 minutes, then beat vigorously with a wooden spoon until the mixture starts to thicken. Stir in the nuts. Continue beating until the mixture takes on a fudge-like consistency. Quickly pour into the prepared pan and let stand in a cool place to set. Cut the fudge into squares to serve.

easy chocolate fudge

makes 25 pieces
prep: 10 mins, plus 🕐
1 hr chilling
cook: 5–10 mins 🕐

*This is the easiest fudge to make—for a really rich flavor,
use a good-quality semisweet chocolate with a high cocoa content,
ideally at least 70 percent.*

INGREDIENTS

2¾ oz/75 g unsalted butter, cut into
even-size pieces, plus extra
for greasing

1 lb 2 oz/500 g semisweet chocolate

14 oz/400 g canned sweetened
condensed milk

½ tsp vanilla extract

variation

Replace the vanilla extract with
1 teaspoon rum. Add the rum with the
butter and condensed milk in Step 1.

cook's tip

If there is any left, you can store
the fudge in an airtight container
in a cool, dry place for up to 1 month.
Do not freeze.

1 Lightly grease an
20-cm/8-inch square
cake pan with butter. Break the
chocolate into small pieces and
place in a large, heavy-bottom
pan with the butter and
condensed milk.

2 Heat gently, stirring
constantly, until the
chocolate and butter melt and
the mixture is smooth. Do not
let boil. Remove from the heat.
Beat in the vanilla extract, then
beat the mixture for a few
minutes until thickened. Pour it
into the pan and level the top.

3 Let the mixture chill in
the refrigerator for
1 hour, or until firm. Tip the
fudge out onto a cutting board
and cut into squares to serve.

chocolate-dipped fruit

serves 4   **prep: 15 mins, plus** ⟳ **30 mins chilling**   **cook: 5 mins** ♨

Fresh fruit dipped in chocolate looks attractive and is less rich than ordinary chocolates, making it an ideal treat to serve with coffee at the end of a heavy meal.

INGREDIENTS

12 large cherries, with stalks attached

12 cape gooseberries

7 oz/200 g semisweet chocolate, broken into pieces

1 tbsp corn oil

variation

Small strawberries would make a good alternative or addition to the cherries and cape gooseberries.

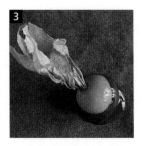

1 Line a baking sheet with nonstick parchment paper. Wash and dry the cherries. Peel back the papery outer case from the cape gooseberries and twist at the top to make a "handle."

2 Place the chocolate and oil in a small heatproof bowl and set over a pan of gently simmering water until the chocolate has melted. Remove from the heat, stir to mix, then let cool until tepid. Dip the fruit in the chocolate and let any excess drain back into the pan. The fruit does not need to be completely coated.

3 Set the fruit on the prepared baking sheet. If the chocolate forms a "foot" on the paper, it is too warm, so let it cool slightly. If the chocolate in the bowl starts to set, warm it gently over the pan of simmering water. Chill the dipped fruit in the refrigerator for 30 minutes, or until the chocolate is set, then peel away from the paper. Serve on their own, or use to decorate another dessert.

chocolate marzipans

⏱ **cook: 10 mins**   ⏱ **prep: 40 mins, plus 2 hrs chilling**   **makes 30**

These delightful little marzipans make the perfect gift, if you can resist eating them all yourself! Alternatively, arrange on a serving plate and serve with coffee as an after-dinner treat.

variation

Coat the marzipan balls in white or milk chocolate and drizzle with semisweet chocolate, if you prefer.

INGREDIENTS

1 lb/450 g marzipan

generous ⅛ cup candied cherries, very finely chopped

confectioners' sugar, for dusting

generous ⅛ cup preserved ginger, very finely chopped

generous ¼ cup no-soak dried apricots, very finely chopped

12 oz/350 g semisweet chocolate, broken into pieces

1 oz/25 g white chocolate

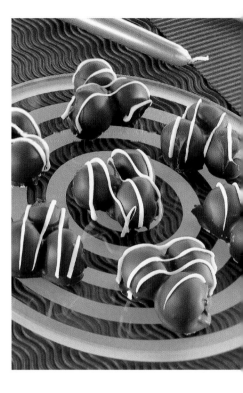

1 Line a baking sheet with nonstick parchment paper. Divide the marzipan into 3 balls and knead each ball to soften it.

2 Work the candied cherries into 1 portion of the marzipan by kneading on a counter lightly dusted with confectioners' sugar. Do the same with the preserved ginger and another portion of marzipan, then the apricots and the third portion of marzipan. Form each flavored portion of marzipan into small balls, keeping the flavors separate.

3 Place the semisweet chocolate in a heatproof bowl and set over a pan of hot water. Stir until the chocolate has melted. Dip one of each flavored ball of marzipan into the melted chocolate by spiking each one with a toothpick, allowing the excess chocolate to drip back into the bowl.

4 Place the balls in clusters of the 3 flavors on the baking sheet. Repeat with the remaining balls. Let chill in the refrigerator for 1 hour, or until set. Place the white chocolate in a small heatproof bowl and set over a pan of simmering water. Stir until the chocolate has melted. Drizzle a little over the tops of each cluster of marzipan balls. Let chill in the refrigerator for 1 hour, or until hard. Remove from the parchment paper, arrange on a plate and serve.

apricot & almond clusters

cook: 5 mins   **prep: 10 mins, plus 2–4 hrs setting**   **makes 24–28**

These delicious little candies are extremely quick and easy to make.
They are perfect for an after-dinner treat with coffee.

variation

Dates would also work well in this recipe. Substitute the apricots with the same amount of chopped, no-soak dates.

cook's tip

These are easy candies for children to make, as long as they have some help with melting the chocolate.

INGREDIENTS

4 oz/115 g semisweet chocolate, broken Into pieces

2 tbsp honey

⅔ cup no-soak dried apricots, chopped

¾ cup blanched almonds, chopped

1 Place the chocolate and honey in a heatproof bowl and set over a pan of gently simmering water until the chocolate has melted.

2 Stir the apricots and almonds into the melted chocolate mixture.

3 Drop teaspoonfuls of the mixture into petit four cases. Let set for 2–4 hours, or until firm. Serve.

torrone molle

makes 24 pieces   **prep: 30 mins, plus 8 hrs chilling**   **cook: 15 mins**

This is a delicious Italian speciality, which is a rich mixture of good-quality semisweet chocolate, ground nuts, and plain cookies.

INGREDIENTS

oil, for brushing

6 oz/175 g butter, softened

6 oz/175 g semisweet chocolate, melted (see pages 9–10)

½ cup shelled walnuts, coarsely ground

⅜ cup blanched almonds, coarsely ground

⅜ cup shelled hazelnuts, coarsely ground

scant ⅔ cup golden superfine sugar

3 tbsp water

1 tbsp brandy

6 oz/175 g plain cookies, such as Petit Beurre

variation

If you like, substitute rum for the brandy and ground pecan nuts for the ground hazelnuts.

cook's tip

If you are grinding the nuts yourself in a food processor, take care not to overprocess them or they will become too oily and may spoil the finished dish.

1 Brush an 11 x 8-inch/ 28 x 20-cm jelly roll pan with oil. Place the softened butter in a bowl, add the melted chocolate, and beat together until smooth. Stir in the walnuts, almonds, and hazelnuts. Place the sugar and water in a heavy-bottom pan and heat until the sugar has dissolved.

2 Boil the mixture steadily until a temperature of 241°F/116°C has been reached on a sugar thermometer, or a small amount of the mixture forms a soft ball when dropped into cold water. Let cool for a few minutes, then beat vigorously. Pour into the chocolate mixture, stirring constantly, until smooth.

3 Stir in the brandy. Break the cookies into small almond-size pieces and stir gently into the mixture. Turn into the prepared pan and press to flatten. Cover and let chill in the refrigerator for 8 hours, or overnight. Remove from the refrigerator just before serving and cut into diamond shapes.

mini chocolate cones

makes 10   **prep: 40 mins, plus 3–4 hrs chilling**   **cook: 5 mins**

These unusual cone-shaped mint-cream chocolates make a change from the more usual cup shape, and are perfect as an after-dinner chocolate with coffee or liqueurs.

INGREDIENTS

2¾ oz/75 g semisweet chocolate

generous ⅓ cup heavy cream

1 tbsp confectioners' sugar

1 tbsp crème de menthe

chocolate-covered coffee beans,
to decorate (optional)

cook's tip

The chocolate cones can be made in advance and kept in the refrigerator for up to 1 week. Do not fill them more than 2 hours before you are going to serve them.

1 Cut 10 x 3-inch/7.5-cm circles of parchment paper. Shape each circle into a cone shape and secure with a piece of sticky tape.

2 Break the chocolate into pieces, place in a heatproof bowl, and set over a pan of hot water. Stir until the chocolate has melted.

Using a small pastry brush or clean artists' brush, brush the inside of each cone with the melted chocolate.

3 Brush a second layer of chocolate on the inside of the cones and let chill in the refrigerator for 2 hours, or until set. Carefully peel away the paper.

4 Place the cream, confectioners' sugar and crème de menthe in a large bowl and whip until just holding its shape. Place in a pastry bag fitted with a star tip and pipe the mixture into the chocolate cones.

5 Decorate the cones with chocolate-covered coffee beans, if using, and let chill in the refrigerator for 1–2 hours, until required.

brazil nut brittle

⏲ **cook: 10 mins**   ⏱ **prep: 20 mins, plus 30 mins setting**   **makes 20**

Chunks of fudge, white chocolate, and Brazil nuts are embedded in semisweet chocolate. For the best results, choose the highest-quality chocolate that you can find.

cook's tip

Put the brittle on a serving plate or in an airtight container and keep, covered, in a cool place. Alternatively, you can store it in the refrigerator for up to 3 days.

INGREDIENTS

oil, for brushing

12 oz/350 g semisweet chocolate, broken into pieces

scant ¾ cup shelled Brazil nuts, chopped

6 oz/175 g white chocolate, coarsely chopped

6 oz/175 g fudge, coarsely chopped

1 Brush the bottom of a 8-inch/20-cm square cake pan with oil and line with parchment paper. Melt half the semisweet chocolate (see pages 9–10) and spread in the prepared pan.

2 Sprinkle with the chopped Brazil nuts, white chocolate, and fudge. Melt the remaining semisweet chocolate pieces and pour over the top.

3 Let the brittle set, then break up into jagged pieces using the tip of a strong knife.

quick chocolate milk shake

serves 2   **prep: 5 mins**   **cook: 0 mins**

This is a great way to encourage children to drink milk, although adults will also enjoy this drink.

INGREDIENTS

6 rounded tbsp vanilla ice cream

4 tbsp drinking chocolate

1¼ cups milk

1 chocolate flake bar, coarsely crushed

ground cinnamon, for dusting

variation

For a more chocolatey milk shake, use chocolate ice cream instead of vanilla, and decorate the top with a light dusting of unsweetened cocoa.

1 Place the vanilla ice cream, drinking chocolate, and milk in a blender or food processor.

2 Process the mixture for 30 seconds, then pour into 2 tall serving glasses.

3 Sprinkle with the flake, add a light dusting of cinnamon, and serve with straws, if you like.

real hot chocolate

cook: 5 mins   **prep: 5 mins**   **serves 1–2**

You will never go back to commercial drinking chocolate once you have tasted this! Choose the best-quality chocolate you can buy.

variation

Chocolate powder for dusting on cappuccino is available in most large supermarkets alongside the coffee. Alternatively, use drinking chocolate or unsweetened cocoa.

INGREDIENTS

1½ oz/40 g semisweet chocolate, broken into pieces

1¼ cups milk

2 tbsp whipped cream, to decorate

chocolate powder, for dusting

1 Place the chocolate in a large, heatproof measuring cup. Place the milk in a heavy-bottom pan and bring to a boil. Pour about one-quarter of the milk onto the chocolate and leave until the chocolate has softened.

2 Whisk the milk and chocolate mixture until smooth. Return the remaining milk to the heat and bring back to a boil, then pour onto the chocolate, whisking constantly.

3 Pour into warmed mugs or cups and top with whipped cream dusted with chocolate powder. Serve immediately.

mexicana

serves 2   **prep: 5 mins**   **cook: 0 mins**

Chocolate, coffee, and rum make this a drink to lift the spirits. It looks particularly attractive served in tall, heatproof glasses.

INGREDIENTS

1 oz/25 g semisweet chocolate

1¼ cups hot black coffee

2 tbsp golden superfine sugar

1 tbsp rum

TO DECORATE

2 tbsp whipped cream

ground coffee

---

variation

If your time is limited, you can use ready-to-serve whipped cream, which is sold in cans. Just shake the can well, squirt on top of the drink and serve.

1 Place the chocolate, coffee, and sugar in a blender or food processor.

2 Process until well blended, then add the rum, stir, and pour into 2 tall, heatproof glasses.

3 Top with whipped cream and sprinkle with a little ground coffee. Serve immediately.

chocolate eggnog

cook: 5 mins　　　　**prep: 15 mins**　　　　**serves 4**

The perfect pick-me-up on a cold winter's night, this delicious drink will get the taste buds tingling.

cook's tip

If you don't have any rum, then you can use brandy instead. Try to use a good-quality semisweet chocolate for grating over the drink.

INGREDIENTS

8 egg yolks

1 cup sugar

4 cups milk

8 oz/225 g semisweet chocolate, grated

⅔ cup dark rum

1 Place the egg yolks and sugar in a large bowl and, using an electric mixer, mix until thickened.

2 Pour the milk into a large, heavy-bottom pan, add the grated semisweet chocolate and bring to a boil.

3 Remove the pan from the heat and gradually mix into the egg yolk mixture. Stir in the rum, pour into heatproof glasses, and serve immediately.

hot brandy chocolate

serves 4   **prep: 10 mins**   **cook: 7–10 mins**

Brandy and chocolate have a natural affinity with one another, as this richly flavored drink amply demonstrates.

INGREDIENTS

4 cups milk

4 oz/115 g semisweet chocolate, broken into pieces

2 tbsp sugar

5 tbsp brandy

TO DECORATE

6 tbsp whipped cream

4 tsp unsweetened cocoa

cook's tip

When melting chocolate and milk, always use a heavy-bottom pan and stir constantly to prevent the chocolate and milk burning on the bottom of the pan.

1 Pour the milk into a large, heavy-bottom pan and bring to a boil over low heat. As soon as it reaches boiling point, remove the pan from the heat.

2 Place the chocolate in a small pan and add 2 tablespoons of the milk. Stir over low heat until the chocolate has melted, then stir the chocolate mixture into the remaining milk. Add the sugar.

3 Stir in the brandy and pour into 4 tall, heatproof glasses. Top each with a swirl of whipped cream and sprinkle with a little sifted unsweetened cocoa. Serve immediately.

café mocha

⏱ **cook: 5 mins**　　　　⏲ **prep: 5 mins**　　　　**serves 2**

This is sheer indulgence for coffee- and chocolate-lovers alike. Choose the best quality ice cream, or even make your own.

---

variation

For a change, replace the coffee ice cream with chocolate or vanilla ice cream, if you like.

INGREDIENTS

2 oz/55 g semisweet chocolate, broken into pieces

2 tbsp water

2 tbsp golden superfine sugar

1 cup milk

½ cup freshly made strong black coffee

2 scoops of coffee ice cream

2 tbsp whipped cream, to decorate (optional)

1 Place the chocolate, water, and sugar in a heavy-bottom pan and heat gently until melted. Stir until smooth. Set aside a little of the sauce for decoration.

2 Stir the milk into the chocolate sauce. Divide the coffee between 2 warmed glasses and pour the chocolate mixture over.

3 Add the ice cream and drizzle the reserved chocolate sauce over. Top each glass with a tablespoonful of cream, if you like, and serve.

index

index

index